Push Beyond Your Limits

How to Develop the Grit, Drive, and Hustle to Make Your Entrepreneurial Goals a Success

Published by
Hybrid Global Publishing
333 E 14th Street
#3C
New York, NY 10003

Manufactured in the United States of America, or in the United Kingdom when distributed elsewhere.

Martin, Dr. Teresa.
Push Beyond Your Limits
     ISBN: 978-1-957013-88-6
     eBook: 978-1-957013-89-3
     LCCN: 2023911062

Cover design by: Natasha Clawson
Copyediting by: Wendie Perchasky
Interior design by: Suba Murugan

enjoyyourlegacy.com

CONTENTS

FOREWORD

Linda Clemons®

Growth comes from pushing beyond the limits of what's possible within the context of your available competencies and personal resources. However, the challenge for so many aspiring entrepreneurs is that they don't always know how to effectively call upon that reservoir of strength and fortitude that oftentimes lies beneath adversity.

In this amazing book, *Push Beyond Your Limits*, Dr. Teresa R. Martin, Esq., shares her own groundbreaking journey of transformation, growth, and courage in the face of seemingly insurmountable odds. To effectively participate in economic activities and, more importantly, make appropriate financial decisions, Dr. Teresa declares that both men and women need to be sufficiently financially literate.

When we fully understand the stark contrast of the wealth gap in our society, Dr. Teresa's book becomes an urgent call for us to transform our thinking. For every one dollar of wealth held by a White family, a Black family had just twenty-five cents in 2022, according to the Federal Reserve Bank of St. Louis. Black people have always faced unique barriers to creating our wealth. From homeownership to business ownership, historical factors have always been aligned against us.

To work toward closing the racial wealth gap and building generational wealth for Black Americans, it's important to understand what obstacles stand in the way. Through her own transformational journey, Dr. Teresa provides a roadmap for the construction of building generational wealth. Through the pathway of business enterprise, we can learn how to create the tomorrow we are so desperately searching for.

A true servantpreneur, Dr. Teresa has become the vessel through which her ministry of serving others can unfold. Hers is a life formulated through a unique combination of stewardship, servant leadership, and marketing ministry.

Demonstrating her amazing ability to pivot, Dr. Teresa adapted quickly to the rapidly changing business landscape brought about by the COVID-19 pandemic. Even amid the backdrop of economic gloom, recession, unemployment, and business failures, Dr. Teresa sought refuge through the creation of new enterprises as she assisted clients to navigate massive technological revolution.

Push Beyond Your Limits is an entrepreneur's playbook on how to face disruptions head-on and rise above them. Distinctively different, *Push Beyond Your Limits* is hosted by a leader in her field that knows how to walk the talk and has a litany of clients who cite her as being instrumental in either shaping their businesses or helping them to turn their fortunes around.

The rich principles cited in this book are brought to life through the real-life examples of the featured authors, providing an analytical framework that any entrepreneur can use to transform crises into opportunities.

Entrepreneurs must continue to evolve and transform to stay relevant in an ever-changing landscape. Dr. Teresa displays an extraordinary knowledge of the legal, real estate, and business world and has brought together inspiring entrepreneurs in many industries who share their wisdom on the pages of this book.

Whether you are a leader, an entrepreneur running a multi-national corporation, or even an upstart, make the most of the anecdotal jewels that are to be found in this book. I guarantee you will be inspired to not only seize the challenges that are before you but develop pathways yet to be uncovered.

Linda Clemons® is a global sales and nonverbal communications expert. The CEO of Sisterpreneur® Inc. of Indianapolis, Indiana, Linda is a charismatic speaker and corporate trainer with more than three decades of experience. She provides sales and leadership teams with an awareness of how body language can improve performance and boost sales.

www.lindaclemonsebooks.com

INTRODUCTION

Dr. Teresa R. Martin

As a woman in the workforce, you may be finding it challenging to balance your professional and personal life while also pursuing your entrepreneurial dreams. The struggle to find time, resources, and support can be overwhelming, leading to feelings of being overworked and underappreciated. The demands of balancing a career with personal responsibilities can take a toll on your physical and mental health, leaving you feeling drained and unmotivated.

Sleep deprivation, stress, and the fear of failure can all contribute to a feeling of being stuck in the same place with no way out. As a female entrepreneur, you face a unique set of obstacles that can stand in your way of financial freedom and success in the corporate world. According to a recent study, women face a significant gender gap when it comes to startup funding, with only 3 percent of venture capital funding going toward female-led companies. This lack of financial support can lead to a lack of resources, perpetuating the cycle of struggle and discouragement.

Furthermore, women often face discrimination and bias in the workforce that hinders their professional progress. This can include gender-based pay disparities, limited opportunities for promotions, and cultural and societal expectations that prioritize family and caregiving responsibilities over career advancement.

These challenges make it difficult to balance the demands of work and personal life, leading to a sense of burnout and exhaustion.

Despite these challenges, it is important to remember that you are not alone. Many successful women have faced similar obstacles and have gone on to achieve their dreams. Mother Teresa said, "We need to find God, and he cannot be found in noise and restlessness. God is the friend of silence. See how nature—trees, flowers, grass—grows in silence; see the stars, the moon, and the sun, how they move in silence. . . . We need silence to be able to touch souls." This means that even when times are hard or you feel like giving up on something you believe in, take some time to be still and remember what matters most. Taking Mother Teresa's advice, we can push beyond our limits.

With the right mindset, tools, and support network, you too can overcome the barriers that stand in your way and create a fulfilling and rewarding career. That's exactly what this book is about—it's meant to guide, motivate, and support women like you.

This book serves as an invaluable resource to provide you with the necessary knowledge, support, and motivation to help you take charge of your own destiny. You'll understand the unique obstacles women face when starting their own business or investing in real estate, from technological hurdles to fee competition. It also offers guidance on how to create achievable goals and how to handle personal hardships along with work-related stressors. Finally, it shows you how you can prioritize your health and wellness while making progress toward your entrepreneurial dreams.

Becoming an entrepreneur can be daunting for anyone, but for women who already have a job, the task can seem insurmountable. However, there are countless examples of motivated entrepreneurs who have faced these challenges head-on and succeeded. You'll meet some of these inspiring souls in the pages of *Push Beyond Your Limits*. These entrepreneurs have shared their experiences and provide valuable lessons for those who dare to take the leap.

As someone who has succeeded in finding fulfillment in her career, I empathize with the apprehension and anxieties that accompany starting a business. I chose to remain within the legal field, but I was determined to practice law in a manner that would bring me satisfaction, offer a healthy work-life balance, and genuinely support my clients. It was a difficult journey that consumed over a decade and required expenditures of hundreds of thousands of dollars. However, the tragic events of 9/11 confirmed that I had made the right decision.

Throughout my journey of creating a new business model, I often doubted myself and questioned if it was worth the investment. But I knew I wasn't alone in my desire for something better. There were other women entrepreneurs out there who longed for a successful business without sacrificing their personal lives. I aimed to pave the way for them so they, too, could realize their dreams without having to start from scratch.

When doubts crept in, I reminded myself that every step I took was not just for myself and my family but for all the other women in the same position I had been in. I was determined to lead the way and offer a solution for those who have struggled with the traditional business model. I knew that my actions would help other entrepreneurs escape the same difficulties and find success a lot quicker than I did. With that thought in mind, I persevered through the long years and countless investments.

My road to success was not easy. I often questioned whether I could make a difference and achieve my goals, just like so many of you. But through perseverance, trial and error, and an unwavering belief in myself, I have made significant strides in my career and personal life.

I eventually created the Fiscally Fabulous® Business Model, a proven approach that can help you achieve both personal and financial freedom. It is all about utilizing your unique experiences and skills to create a business that brings you joy, meaning, and financial stability. With this model, you have the ability to control your schedule and your income, while providing a valuable service to your clients.

This collection of lessons from successful thought leaders and entrepreneurs will help you understand what it takes to succeed as an entrepreneur. *Push Beyond Your Limits: How to Develop the Grit, Drive, and Hustle to Make Your Entrepreneurial Goals a Success* shares inspiring stories from entrepreneurs who have overcome obstacles and fear while pursuing their dreams. These successful entrepreneurs have faced similar struggles as you, including overcoming traditional business model limitations and personal challenges. These men and women want to offer reassurance and inspire you to pursue your goals.

Each entrepreneur has a unique message to share real-life experiences of overcoming financial difficulties, fear, and other obstacles that threatened to hinder them. Moreover, they offer valuable insights into how they conquered these challenges and provide essential lessons on building a successful business.

For example, one of the contributing entrepreneurs, William Moore, reflects on his own experience of doubting his capabilities: "I used to think that I wasn't cut out for entrepreneurship—that it was too risky and success was only for certain types of people. But I learned that the only person holding me back was me. Once I started taking small steps toward my dream, I realized that I was capable of so much more than I ever imagined."

As you read and learn from these remarkable entrepreneurs, let yourself be inspired and motivated. "Ask and it will be given to you; seek and you will find; knock and the door will be opened to you" (Matthew 7:7).

Additionally, this book will teach you how to use your time wisely, meet new people, manage your money, and change the way you think. All these lessons will help you on your journey to become a successful entrepreneur.

At the end of the day, success in entrepreneurship is possible if you have grit and hustle. The inspiring stories from the entrepreneurs featured in this book will provide a roadmap for how to overcome obstacles and achieve your goals. So don't wait any longer—turn the page, start reading, and begin this empowering journey today!

If you would like to meet like-minded entrepreneurs and business leaders like the authors in this book, they are all members of an unique and powerful collaborative organization called Enjoy Your Legacy.

Learn more at www.EnjoyYourLegacy.com

DELAYED IS NOT DENIED: MY ROAD TO "SUCCESS"

LaVonne Barksdale

Life is like a roller-coaster ride. It has twists and turns, sometimes taking you to dizzying heights of success and other times plunging you into the depths of failure. It's easy to get stuck in the valleys when life throws unexpected curves at us. But for those who are determined enough, even the most daunting obstacles can be overcome with resilience and hard work.

Dreams Deferred
What happens to a dream deferred?
Does it dry up
Like a raisin in the sun?
Or fester like a sore
And then run?
Does it stink like rotten meat
Or crust and sugar over
Like syrupy sweet?
Maybe it just sags
Like a heavy load
Or does it explode

—Langston Hughes

The worthiest of journeys are often filled with overwhelming obstacles and deferred dreams. As Langston Hughes's poem suggests, dreams can be deferred and put on hold for a variety of reasons. But that doesn't mean they are forgotten or lost forever. It's like trying to build a house from the ground up—it takes time, patience, and lots of hard work. Just as constructing a building requires careful planning and attention to detail, so does achieving success in any field. And this is especially true for someone who has had to battle their way through life since childhood like I did.

According to Chris Melore, only 43 percent of adults reported that they are currently living their dreams, and the number further dropped to 19 percent when surveying those who had given up on their dreams.[1] Additionally, another survey conducted by the Gallup organization in 2013 revealed that nearly two-thirds of people in the U.S. have already killed their lifelong dream or don't even have one. These figures clearly demonstrate that not enough people are actively pursuing and achieving their most desired aspirations.

In this chapter, I will take you with me on my voyage, one that goes from early struggles to eventual triumphs as I overcame every obstacle along the way with sheer determination and resilience. I was born and raised in a difficult family environment with nothing more than a dream of one day becoming an established businesswoman. This would not be an easy task, as I quickly learned. My journey was far from linear; I stumbled upon many detours along the way that tested my patience, strength, and courage. This story is for anyone who has ever had a dream deferred and is looking for the strength to keep pushing.

---

[1] Chris Melore, "43% of Americans Say They're Working Their 'Dream Job' from Childhood," September 20, 2021, Study Finds, https://studyfinds.org/childhood-dream-job-americans/.

The Early Years

From my earliest memories until around the age of seven, I lived under a cloud of fear, perpetuated by an unpredictable and violent alcoholic father. Our nights were often spent in uncertainty, wondering whether we could sleep peacefully or have to flee our home, sometimes without shoes, to ensure our safety. Envisioning a future seemed impossible when faced with such constant turmoil.

My family consisted of dedicated city employees. My mother managed SNAP, my grandmother supervised an elementary school lunchroom, my grandfather was the first African American foreman in sanitation, and my aunt transitioned from a public schoolteacher to principal. As the eldest daughter, grandchild, and niece, an enormous weight rested on my shoulders to set an example for those who would follow in my footsteps. For my family, that meant attending college and securing a better city job.

I wasn't discouraged, but when the people you admire don't venture beyond their familiar paths, it's challenging to imagine yourself doing anything different. Breaking free from these expectations required a conscious decision to forge my own path, even if the "how" remained elusive for some time. Eventually, I embarked on my unique journey, discovering my own potential and aspirations much later than I anticipated.

In the words of Sunday Adelaja, "The secret of all greatness is to discover what you were born to do in life and then do it. You must find out your gifts and talents." This quote resonates with me; it emphasizes the importance of breaking free from expectations and venturing beyond familiar paths, discovering courage, and finding your passion regardless of what anyone else thinks.

Unexpected Turns: Where I Was to Where Am I Now

Throughout my educational journey, I excelled in gifted and talented programs, taking great pride in my intelligence. However, upon entering high school, I faced an unexpected challenge. To remain in the gifted program, I needed a score of 91, but one teacher, for reasons unknown, decided to give me a 90. This single point cost me my place in the program, marking the beginning of a period in my life when I felt disillusioned and indifferent toward my future, as it seemed that others were controlling my destiny.

In an episode of *The Tony Robbins Podcast*, Tony Robbins himself said, "People who fail focus on what they have to go through; people who succeed focus on what it will feel like at the end." While external factors may sometimes seem to control our destiny, it is ultimately our response to these situations that shapes our future.

During this time, I met my high school sweetheart, and we shared many wonderful moments together. Despite the setbacks, I managed to graduate with a regents diploma, and I enrolled in the Borough of Manhattan Community College (BMCC) to study nursing. However, after some time, I realized that nursing wasn't the right path for me.

This realization prompted me to reevaluate my goals and aspirations, seeking a new direction that would align with my passions and strengths. The journey wasn't easy, but it taught me valuable lessons about resilience, adaptability, and the importance of taking charge of my own destiny, even when faced with obstacles and setbacks.

Fast-forward to the present day, and I'm now working for the city of New York as the director of the Landlord Management Unit (LMU), with approximately seven years left until retirement. Though I followed in my family's footsteps by pursuing a career within the city, I also managed to achieve something none of them had—establishing my own businesses.

Today, I wear multiple hats as a real estate agent, mentor, Multiple Listing Service (MLS) instructor, and emerging property investor. Furthermore, I have founded a not-for-profit organization called The Barksdale Transitional Group, LLC. This organization is dedicated to providing housing and support to homeless veterans, with a vision to eventually offer transitional services, career assistance, and other resources to help those who have selflessly served our country.

Through determination and perseverance, I have been able to create a fulfilling life that not only encompasses my city career but also allows me to make a meaningful impact through my entrepreneurial ventures and philanthropic efforts.

All in Between: From Shackles to the Rise

My decision to attend community college was largely influenced by my rebellious feelings and dissatisfaction with my unfair removal from the gifted and talented program. During this time, my mother insisted that I find a job. I began working at a check-cashing establishment before eventually securing a position as a bank teller in 1988.

At that point in my life, I was living with my boyfriend, who regrettably became abusive and quit his job, leaving me responsible for our household expenses. We lived together for only three months in a small room with a shared bathroom and kitchen, which was also home to an unwelcome rat. Unable to tolerate the unhealthy living conditions and my boyfriend's behavior, I decided to leave.

Returning to my mother's house, I soon discovered that I was pregnant with my son. At the age of twenty, I chose to keep him and determinedly embraced the challenge of figuring out how to provide for our future. This pivotal moment in my life marked the beginning of a journey filled with resilience, personal growth, and the unwavering determination to create a better life for myself and my child.

During this period, I reconnected with my high school sweetheart, and we resumed our relationship for another five to six years. Together, we welcomed a daughter into the world when

I was twenty-two years old. My high school sweetheart lovingly embraced the role of a father to both my daughter and my son, who had been abandoned by his biological father mere days after his birth.

While my children's father served in the military, sending money home to support us, I chose to stay home and care for our family. However, to make ends meet and provide for our needs, I found it necessary to rely on public assistance during that time. The experience of raising my children under these circumstances taught me invaluable lessons about resilience, resourcefulness, and the importance of keeping the family together through thick and thin.

When my son was four and my daughter three, they attended Head Start, conveniently located next to my city job as a clerk. I worked in various positions over the next years, all with increasing levels of responsibility and consistent promotions, including stints in Medicaid, the Human Resources Administration, and the Department of Homeless Services. Today, I hold the position of director of the Landlord Management Unit, which I have been leading since March 2021. My journey through various roles and departments has equipped me with a wealth of knowledge and experience, shaping me into the dedicated professional I am today.

Ladder to Success

While juggling my professional responsibilities, I pursued my passion for real estate and obtained my license in 2017. However, fear of starting initially held me back, causing me to hesitate until 2019. I've always had an entrepreneurial spirit, although it initially took a back seat due to my struggles with self-doubt and perfectionism.

As Chris Guillebeau once said, "The best time to start was last year. Failing that, today will do." This quote eventually inspired me to take the leap. With some help, I was able to overcome my fear and embark on my real estate journey.

Life threw in another setback in February 2019, when I underwent major back surgery. As I recovered, I decided to seize the opportunity and give real estate a try while I was temporarily out of work. I started with Exit Realty, but their beliefs did not align with mine, and I found it challenging to establish my business. In November 2019, I joined eXp Realty, just as I was beginning to find my footing in the industry. Unfortunately, the pandemic struck, and our ability to conduct business was severely impacted.

However, the pandemic also brought about unexpected opportunities. The city allowed us to work from home, which I did for almost two years. This newfound flexibility eliminated my commute to and from my Manhattan office, freeing up valuable time I could devote to my real estate business. I was able to attend more showings, participate in trainings, and follow up with clients more efficiently.

I used the challenges presented by the pandemic as a catalyst for growth and success in my real estate career. Throughout my career, I have been committed to continuous learning and self-improvement, recognizing that knowledge is the key to success in the real estate industry. To stay informed on best practices and emerging trends, I have read countless books, attended numerous seminars (both in-person and virtual), participated in mastermind groups, and forged valuable relationships with fellow professionals.

Since joining eXp Realty, my earnings have shown significant growth, demonstrating the impact of my dedication and hard work:

- In 2019, I earned $5,050.
- In 2021, my earnings skyrocketed to $1,445,186.

- As of now, my current earnings stand at $1,397,000, and my cap doesn't reset until November 2023.

This impressive progress serves as a testament to the power of perseverance, passion, and the relentless pursuit of knowledge.

As the renowned motivational speaker Zig Ziglar once said, "You don't have to be great to start, but you have to start to be great." By taking the initial leap into the real estate world and continually seeking opportunities for growth and development, I have been able to achieve remarkable success in my career.

Takeaways from My Journey That Will Help You

- *Don't let societal expectations define who you are and what you should do with your life.* There is beauty in being different, so don't be afraid to explore new paths and take risks along the way.
- *Establish a strong social media presence from the outset.* Platforms such as Facebook, Instagram, TikTok, and YouTube can help you connect with potential clients and showcase your expertise. Consistency in posting content, including videos and articles, is crucial for building an engaged audience.
- *Regularly follow up with both prospective and current clients, even when there are no specific updates to share.* Maintaining communication demonstrates your commitment and ensures they know they have not been forgotten.
- *Effective time management is essential for success in the real estate business.* Allocate dedicated time for prospecting and avoid interruptions from emails or phone calls during this period.

- *Keep track of your clients and the various stages of their deals.* As your business grows, you will likely have multiple transactions in progress simultaneously, making it vital to stay organized.
- *Consider subscribing to lead generation services to kickstart your business by connecting with potential clients.*
- *After completing a deal, request a review from your client.* Reviews play a significant role in influencing others' decisions, especially for high-stakes transactions such as property purchases. By gathering positive reviews, you can build trust and credibility with future clients.
- *Embrace the role of a humble agent.* It's important to acknowledge that you may not have all the answers, and it's perfectly acceptable to inform your clients that you will research their query and get back to them with accurate information, rather than providing an incorrect response.
- *Keep in mind that while this industry can be financially rewarding, its true essence lies in being a people-oriented business.* Your primary focus should be delivering exceptional, personalized service to each client. By adopting the philosophy of prioritizing people over profits, you'll not only earn the trust of your clients but also gain valuable referrals from their friends and family, as they'll inevitably think of you whenever someone mentions purchasing a home.

Finally, in the journey of life, our dreams are the crucial elements that connect our hopes, ambitions, and passions. They fuel our inner drive, pushing us to tirelessly chase after what we truly want. It's essential never to give up on these dreams, even when faced with tough obstacles or daunting challenges. There may be times when we need to put our dreams on hold temporarily to adapt to unexpected changes in life, but we should always stay true to their core.

LaVonne Barksdale is the director of a Homelessness Prevention Administration program, the Landlord Management Unit (LMU). She is a licensed Realtor, an instructor with Hudson Gateway Association of Realtors (HGAR) Multiple Listing Service (MLS), and the founder of VerteranSpeak, which serves homeless veterans. She currently resides in New York and is the proud mother of two.

www.buildingit-together.com

STAND FIRM WHEN LIFE THROWS YOU A CURVEBALL

Natacha Ferrari and Sandra Ferrari

We've been running the New York City Marathon since 2003, and after finishing each one, we would take a vacation outside of the United States. We figure that after spending months of training, we ought to celebrate after completing the race. So, in November 2008, after completing the 39th Annual New York City Marathon, we were elated to be part of the 37,790 runners who finished the race that day. Paula Radcliffe, the fastest and most amazing British female runner in the world at that time, won the race. We felt as if we were on top of the world that November. Little did we know that life was about to throw us a curveball that would turn our world upside down.

Sandra

My fraternal twin sister and I did not expect this curveball to hit us with such force. Upon returning from vacation, quietly, without fanfare, without a thank you, Natacha told me that her entire real estate unit at the Related Companies had been dismissed. No one was aware that the company had been severely impacted by the Great Recession of 2008.

Once I heard what had transpired that day, a sadness enveloped me. Admittedly, I was more concerned about losing the house and not being able to pay the bills than my sister's feelings. It was our combined income that paid the mortgage, the monthly expenses, and the other debts. To add insult to injury, Natacha's salary was higher than mine at the time.

I was petrified. I was angry. I was scared. I was aware of the economic issues the country was facing, but I never imagined it would affect my family directly. The collapse of the housing market was real and tangible. Our American dream was crumbling before our eyes.

Being a faithful woman, I turned to God, but still I felt incomplete. I suffered through a severe desolation period with no end in sight. I was afraid that we would become pariahs before our family and friends. My fear of losing our house increased even more. Natacha, on the other hand, seemed unaffected by this situation. I accused her many times of adopting a laissez-faire attitude. In my eyes, she didn't seem to care.

Every day, when I went to work at my firm, my boss constantly reminded us that we had to push cases to trial, or we wouldn't have any money to keep the business afloat or receive any bonuses. Thoughts of losing my job loomed over me. My fear of losing everything began to paralyze me. I couldn't think logically.

Natacha

Ten years earlier, my sister and I, just a few year out of college, purchased a beautiful single-family home. At our housewarming party, so many of our friends and family who attended the event congratulated us. Some reminded us that we were living the American dream. And now we were faced with a challenging time that threatened our daily life.

After the November 2008 event, the atmosphere at home became unpleasant. All my sister saw was doomsday, when the house would be foreclosed on. Her fears extended to my thoughts as well. What would people think of us? How would we survive this humiliation? All these thoughts kept recurring in my mind. I was unable to sleep, and I developed insomnia.

According to the media, close to six million American families were displaced due to the Great Recession of 2008. Many people lost their jobs and, as a result, were unable to pay their mortgages. Many financial companies experienced financial distress. The federal government tried to implement some programs to alleviate the economic meltdown. Despite this intervention, the economy worsened in 2008. Sadly, by fall 2008, I became part of these statistics.

Sandra

I couldn't pray. I didn't want to pray either. I felt so alone. How could I let anyone know that I was a failure? I even imagined that soon I would be asked to leave my job as well. I was embroiled in a sea of negativity. I was in a ship that was sinking; my legs and arms had turned to lead, and I was unable to swim. My eyes remained wide open as I slowly descended into the abyss.

Natacha and Sandra

After buying the house, Sandra's big sister in her college sorority had strongly suggested that we needed to meet with a financial advisor to look at our portfolio. Robert, the financial advisor, had directed us to save up to six months as an emergency fund just in case of a rainy day. We had heeded his advice. In addition, we held quarterly meetings to review our financial budget. But still we were not prepared for the 2008 economic meltdown.

We both started working full-time when we purchased the house. We learned to sacrifice and save to accomplish the American dream. We had no worries whatsoever that we would not be able to make the payments. We trusted in the Lord that he would provide all that was necessary. We had forgotten that every step we took, every achievement we accomplished, was with the grace of God. God always was there with us, guiding and protecting us. So now as the ship began to sink and the wind started to blow, Natacha and I sat down and held a meaningful and fruitful meeting.

Yes, our attitude needed an adjustment. We needed to pass the blame phase. Bury the hatchet and move on. Hence, we devised a plan to move forward. At the same time, Natacha would continue to send her resume to various agencies. We would continue to save every penny. And most importantly, we both planned to attend self-development seminars. Natacha's task was to research every free self-improvement seminar in and around New York City. Various events for young and ambitious entrepreneurs were unfolding across the city. We took advantage of these gatherings.

We attended a few free Robert Kiyosaki seminars after reading his book *Rich Dad Poor Dad*. We were enthusiastic to be involved in this new enterprise. We joined Kiyosaki's coaching program. We took a wholesaling class, even though this was not the real estate strategy that we desired. We also studied various strategies, including tax lien, tax deeds, and buy and hold. We were strongly encouraged to utilize OPM (other people's money).

Once we completed the coaching sessions with the Kiyosaki's team, we thought we were ready to start investing. However, deep within, we were gripped with fear. Our credit-card debt mounted. We took solace that this was good debt, not bad debt. We learned that education is essential to investing in real estate—that is, investing in yourself. If you are ignorant of a subject, we strongly suggest you learn from a professional. Knowledge is power.

At the end of our coaching sessions, we were told to join the local real estate investment association (REIA) to help us with our endeavors. We presented at one of the REIA NYC meetings held in downtown Manhattan. The atmosphere was warm and friendly, and we felt welcome.

Moreover, during one of these networking sessions at the REIA NYC meetings, we had the opportunity to meet a member of the REIA, Danny, who was planning to visit an investment property of his in Pittsburgh, Pennsylvania. He invited us to join him on a property tour. We seized the opportunity and headed to Pennsylvania. During this visit, we met with Danny's broker, his property management staff, and enjoyed a wonderful meeting at the Chamber of Commerce with some local representatives. It was a fantastic experience. That visit helped us realize our mission: to be housing providers.

Upon returning to New York, my sister and I discussed the possibility of buying properties there. For the first time, we realized that we could truly start investing in real estate. Our dream could come true.

A few days later, Danny followed up with us to see if we liked the visit and if any of the properties fit our criteria. He further mentioned that he had a banker, an attorney, and a broker in line to help if we were earnestly interested in acquiring one of the properties in Pittsburgh. His entire team would be at our disposal. We told him that we were indeed looking forward to collaborating with him and his team. But where would we obtain the money for such an enterprise?

Let's return for a moment to the house we purchased in 1999. Consequently, this house had accumulated equity since that time. We had never refinanced the house. In fact, before the 2008 event, we used to send an extra payment every year to reduce the life of the mortgage. We opted now to refinance our property. With that money, we purchased our first investment property in Pittsburgh, a duplex, followed by a triplex two months later. Yes, we used OPM. We leveraged our home's equity. To date, we still use this strategy to purchase investment properties.

These two twins, who four years earlier were dealing with fear, adjusted their mindsets and took action by acquiring five units. We were on our way to creating another stream of income. We were happy and grateful. We thanked God for sustaining us during our time of need and for always being with us.

Moreover, we continued to attend the REIA NYC meetings led by Dr. Teresa Martin, Esq., and we became familiar with several vendors who also frequented the meetings. Chris Urso, a multifamily investor, was among the vendors who participated at our REIA meetings. His wife, Lisa, also attended the meetings. We took their coaching course and learned more about multifamily investing.

Another vendor that Dr. Martin introduced to the club was a "Done for You Real Estate" group—where a property is gut-rehabbed and then sold to an investor. The program consisted of rehabbing the home, qualifying the investor with a loan, and placing a qualified tenant in the home. In addition, the assigned agent took the time to speak with us about our financial needs and aided us in managing our goals. With his assistance, we were able to invest in stocks and various commodities via a secured trading module.

Through this program, we acquired a fully renovated single family home in 2015. Since we purchased this property, we've rarely had to make any repairs. In fact, we can count how many times to date a repair has had to be made in the house. We still own this property in our portfolio. It's in a suburb of Memphis, Tennessee. The beauty of real estate investing is that sometimes you don't even need to visit the property prior to purchase. We had boots on the ground.

Nowadays, once a week we receive a call, a text, or a letter from investors asking to buy this property from us. Last year we leveraged that property's equity. We acquired a mortgage note and purchased a brand-new mobile home in one of the most prestigious areas in California. Despite the refinancing, we are still cash flowing after we pay the mortgage and the property management fees. Furthermore, we also receive rent from the mobile home tenants.

Natacha

During 2008 to 2015, we were faced with several challenges and hurdles, one after the other. Since my layoff, my twin sister and I have learned quite a lot. It took me two years to obtain a new job on a temporary basis. We discovered that Robert, our then financial advisor, was right. It is imperative to build an emergency fund and have it ready and available for a rainy day.

Sandra

What started as a dark journey forced us to come out of our comfort zone. Our characters were pushed over the limits. Our spirits have been strengthened. Had Natacha not lost her job, we would never have created this new path. Now she considers this experience a blessing in disguise. We are certain that investing in a property would have never crossed our minds. But we were forced to become entrepreneurs overnight by learning to form and develop business ideas and execute them to provide for our future. Seeking different income streams was the furthest thing from our minds.

Natacha and Sandra

Dr. Martin has become a mentor to us ever since we joined the Real Estate Investment Association of New York City. She often says how we can and should coach others due to our experience in real estate. She is aware of our humble beginning, our story, our tribulations. Poor immigrants from a "third-world" country, we worked hard to reach the American dream. We enjoyed life like any other young people, traveling around the world, supporting our family as well as charitable causes close to our hearts, and being involved in our church and community. We were the perfect poster children of immigrants, but the economic downturn that took place in 2008 threatened to destabilize our life. It forced us to face reality and change our mindset.

We've continued to increase our portfolio. In 2016, we acquired a multifamily property in Ohio. After completing the URS Capital Partners course with the Ursos, we were confident that we were ready to consider that multifamily deal. We utilized the resources at hand without reinventing the wheel. The instructions provided to us during our coaching sessions were extremely helpful. We owned this multifamily property for five years and then sold it successfully. The property management company helped us tremendously during the selling of that property.

After 2020, we also became involved in mortgage notes with the help of Jasmine Willois through the Note Assistance Program. Mortgage notes allow you to become "the Bank." One can invest in single family homes, mobile homes, land, multifamily, etc. There is no limit to what one can do while investing in mortgage notes. This is one of the real estate strategies we'd always desired to use in our portfolio.

We have gone through this immense and painful period where all seemed bleak, and we have not only survived but thrived. You can, too, in similar circumstances!

Lessons we have learned through our journey:

- Do not be discouraged if you lose your job or your pay is not enough.
- Stand firm and look for ways to gain your financial freedom.
- Invest in yourself by obtaining an education in real estate investing.
- Obtain a mentor.
- Join your local REIA.

- Talk to like-minded individuals (networking).
- Form a meetup group.
- Partner with fellow investors.
- Do not let fear paralyze you.
- Devise a financial plan and review it monthly.
- Review and adjust your plan midyear if off course.
- As your business begins to grow, surround yourself with professionals to assist you (i.e., do not be your own accountant if you want to protect your assets).

It is imperative to keep reviewing your goals to see if you are reaching your destination. Cultivate your business and stay informed about the financial market. Don't wait to start taking action until you are faced with a situation like ours. Provide for your family's future today by making preparations that could counteract any unforeseen circumstances. It is, after all, your legacy. Certainly, life will throw you curveballs, but if you remain steadfast, life will also show you how to hit a home run.

Natacha Ferrari is an accountant, and **Sandra Ferrari** is an intake manager at a New York City law firm. Both Natacha and Sandra are speakers, coaches, and real estate investors. Long-time members of REIA NYC, the twins use various strategies to acquire properties across the United States and provide housing services to their clientele.

www.twininvestmentcapitalgroup.com

FAITH, FOCUS, FINANCES: TRANSFORMATION DESPITE LIFE'S CHALLENGES

Natoyah Grinnon

Do you have an entrepreneurial dream you are working hard to make a reality? Are you stuck in the corporate world and want to transition into coaching or consulting? Then I'm here to tell you: It is possible!

I know because I've been there. After years of hard work and hustle, my dreams are now becoming a reality. Along the way, I faced obstacles and fears that could have held me back from achieving success. However, with perseverance and determination, I was able to overcome them all. And if I can do it, so can you!

I graduated from Bentley University in 2003 with a bachelor of science degree in computer information systems. Since graduating, I have worked steadily in the corporate world in various roles.

During my tenure, I've had the opportunity to work with several companies across sectors such as life insurance and financial services. In the life insurance domain, I have been involved in creating policy documents, developing requirements for new product offerings, assisting with benefit calculations, and ensuring regulatory compliance.

In the financial services sector, I've assumed various roles, with a primary focus on collaborating with technology to deliver effective solutions for managing diverse aspects of the business. My experiences have ranged from stock lending and foreign exchange (FX) trading to operational risk and control.

In the area of stock lending, I have worked closely with traders and operations personnel to gain deep insights into their business requirements. I have conducted risk assessments and implemented controls to ensure compliance with SOX requirements. In my capacity, I was also responsible for managing specific portions of projects within the group, delivering tailored technological solutions that aligned with the needs of the securities lending desk. This encompassed developing comprehensive functional specifications based on requirements, evaluating risks, and establishing control measures.

As part of my current involvement in operational risk and control, I collaborate with different departments across the organization to establish robust processes and procedures that effectively address potential risks and control gaps. This involves conducting quality assurance activities to ensure compliance with SOX requirements, focusing on long-term debt and regulatory reporting. To ensure seamless implementation, I engage with product owners, lines of businesses, and technologists, fostering effective communication and collaboration throughout the entire process.

Additionally, my experience in FX trading involved managing projects within the group to enhance support for the business workflows. In this capacity, I bring a project management discipline that emphasizes meeting deadlines and maintaining high-quality standards for deliverables.

Apart from my professional career in the corporate world, my entrepreneurial journey began at the young age of ten when I assisted my grandmother to sell her crops at the local farmer's market. This experience gave me an invaluable opportunity to hone my sales skills while also sharpening my math skills and learning how to interact with buyers and fellow small farmers. As I progressed, I ventured into selling various items for special occasions like Valentine's Day and Christmas, as well as crafting handmade greeting cards for birthdays and other events. Over time, this expanded into creating custom wedding invitations, menu cards, and baking wedding cakes for weddings and character-themed birthday cakes.

Except for occasionally making cakes for friends' birthdays, I no longer pursue these ventures professionally. Since 2015 I have been investing in mortgage notes. More recently, since 2022, I have been focusing primarily on tax liens and tax deeds investments.

I have dedicated significant effort to cultivate the drive and skills necessary for entrepreneurial success. Currently, I am transitioning from my corporate career to coaching and consulting, utilizing my expertise and experiences to assist others in their entrepreneurial pursuits.

Confronting Challenges

Life has never been a smooth journey for me; I have encountered numerous challenges in both my personal life and my pursuit of business aspirations. The year 2008 marked a turning point when I faced the harsh reality of being laid off from not just one but two corporate jobs within a short span of time. The financial burden that followed, with the pressure of rent and other expenses still looming, seemed insurmountable.

In 2014, I was laid off again, and in that same year, I decided to pursue my dream of becoming a full-time entrepreneur by establishing an eCommerce store with my then-husband. We traveled to China and Hong Kong, sourcing fashion jewelry as we brought our vision to life.

Life's challenges continued to mount; 2015 brought with it the painful process of filing for divorce. The divorce was finalized in

2016, but during that time I forced my house into foreclosure, a process which started with my husband's refusal to sign a listing agreement with the real estate agent. Despite attempting a short sale with the bank, I had to tell the bank to take the house, which affected my credit score negatively.

Amidst the emotional toll I endured, my faith became my pillar of strength. Through prayer, fasting, and moments of sitting in silence when words failed me, I found solace and the resilience to keep moving forward. Simultaneously, as the divorce took its toll, my savings depleted rapidly to cover the costs associated with the proceedings and other essential living expenses—all while not having an income. As I worked to get back on track, it became clear that further action was necessary in order to secure my financial future and establish stability for the times ahead.

Despite all these setbacks, I refused to let adversity define me. Fueled by an unyielding determination, I remained steadfast in my goal of becoming a full-time entrepreneur. The trials I faced only served to strengthen my resolve and ignite a fire within me to create a prosperous future.

Overcoming Obstacles through Faith and Investment

> *Obstacles are those frightful things you see when you take your eyes off your goal.*
>
> – Henry Ford

I was able to overcome my obstacles through prayer and fasting. I relied on faith and took comfort in knowing that whatever the outcome, God's plan is always perfect, and my purpose would be fulfilled. Fasting provided a humbling and reflective experience for me, giving me the opportunity to take time away from my daily distractions, focus on God and His promises to me, and gain clarity on my life goals. Throughout the process of fasting,

I developed a better understanding of the importance of staying true to myself and trusting in the divine plan for my life.

To help me get closer to my financial goals, I decided to focus on debt strategies such as mortgage notes investing and tax liens/tax deeds investing. By borrowing from my 401K account, I invested $40k, purchasing over thirty tax liens and tax deeds valued at over $1M in just five months, a feat that would not have been possible without taking initiative and facing any associated fears directly.

Moreover, I took steps to restore my credit score, which had decreased drastically to a score of 530 or lower during the divorce and subsequent home foreclosure. The foreclosure's impact on my credit report lasted for seven years. I worked diligently rebuilding my credit by paying off all my credit card debt in full and on time. After all the hard work, I'm proud to say that my credit score has now increased over 780—something unimaginable during the most challenging times!

I am proof that even when life throws you curveballs, there is always a way out if you are brave enough to go after your dreams!

Strategies to Overcome Obstacles

Based on the obstacles shared in my story above, I'd like to offer suggestions to help you overcome your own challenges. Here are my recommendations divided into two categories: personal (using divorce as an example) and professional (becoming an entrepreneur).

Personal Obstacles

When it comes to personal obstacles, it's important to take some time for yourself and focus on healing. It may also be beneficial to seek professional help.

Divorce is a difficult and life-altering experience with a profound effect on all individuals involved. According to DivorceStatistics. org, up to 50 percent of first marriages end in divorce. Common causes include poor communication, financial strain, intimacy issues, built-up resentment, incompatibility, and unforgiveness. There are also potential psychological and behavioral problems for the children involved.

To prevent reaching a point of no return in a marriage, couples can consider a few alternatives. Counseling can improve physical and emotional intimacy between spouses while providing valuable guidance to address issues and strengthen the marriage. Open communication about each other's needs is crucial to avoid unmet expectations and resentment. Spending quality time together, such as date nights or vacations, can foster a better connection. It's also helpful to have married friends for support and accountability so divorce isn't seen as an easy solution. Finally, both spouses should remember that the other is human and mistakes will be made; patience, forgiveness, and understanding is vital for a successful relationship.

Professional Obstacles

How can you transition from the corporate world to become a full-time entrepreneur?

Transitioning from the corporate world to full-time entrepreneurship is both thrilling and intimidating. While it's a challenging leap, it is possible to succeed with commitment and passion. Starting a business can be daunting yet highly fulfilling. As an entrepreneur, you'll encounter risks and pivotal choices that shape the future of your business. You'll also face numerous challenges along the way, such as lack of capital, market competition, time management issues, and work-life balance. However, by employing effective strategies like the ones below, entrepreneurs can overcome these obstacles and achieve sustainable growth.

- ***Understand Your Personal Habits.*** Understanding your own habits and weaknesses is crucial. Be willing to leave your comfort zone and accept constructive criticism from others. Challenge yourself by setting a daily goal to learn something new or engage in activities that previously intimidated you.

- *Set Goals.* You need to set realistic goals for yourself and your business. These goals should be specific, measurable, achievable, relevant and time-bound (SMART). Break larger goals into smaller chunks that are easier to track and manage. This will help you stay focused on long-term priorities while avoiding distractions from minor tasks or details. Moreover, you need to stay motivated and be consistent. This means breaking down daunting tasks into smaller chunks and taking regular breaks throughout the day so that you can stay focused.

- *Create Systems and Automation.* Systems and automation allow you to manage your operations more easily and free up time to focus on higher-level tasks. Automation can also help reduce human errors, save money, and increase productivity. Leverage technology to streamline your business processes. Explore various apps that facilitate task management, team collaboration, and automate routine operations.

- *Surround Yourself with the Right People.* Choose mentors and advisors who can provide guidance, valuable insights, and feedback relevant to your industry. Additionally, having a network of entrepreneurs who understand your journey can be incredibly helpful for both emotional support and practical advice when needed. Attending social gatherings like workshops, webinars, and conferences is an effective way to connect with like-minded individuals and stay updated on market trends. Joining specialized associations can help to expand your professional network and help you gain valuable industry-specific knowledge.

- *Educate Yourself.* There is no age qualification required to become an entrepreneur; the key lies in self-education and a willingness to learn. Continuous up-skilling is crucial for staying competitive and relevant in the market. Engaging in activities like reading books, attending seminars and conferences, taking courses, listening to podcasts, and seeking guidance from experienced entrepreneurs are all valuable for staying informed about best practices, trends, and strategies for success. It's also important to have a solid grasp of essential business skills such as accounting, marketing, sales, customer service etc. Understanding each facet of running a business enables informed decision-making and preparedness for various situations.

- *Let Go of Excessive Control.* Entrepreneurs often have big ideas for their businesses, but sometimes these don't always unfold as expected. Learn to relinquish control over certain projects or processes without micromanaging. Although challenging, effective delegation requires placing trust in those around you.

- *Minimize Distractions.* To enhance productivity, set specific time slots for tasks such as responding to emails, making phone calls, or checking social media. Doing these activities during the same time every day helps to ensure that they never become distractions. For example, allotting one hour in the morning and another hour in the afternoon to respond to emails can help you maintain focus.

- *Stay Positive.* It's natural to occasionally feel discouraged, but it's essential that you stay focused on the long-term vision. Surround yourself with supportive individuals who will encourage you and remind you why you started in the first place.

- *Manage Your Motivation.* While not every day will yield success, each day contributes to the overall process. Being continuously motivated by little wins is just as important as celebrating larger successes so you don't get discouraged when things don't go according to plan.

- *Be an Ambassador for Your Brand.* Understanding your brand inside and out is only half the challenge; being able to address negative reactions or misinformation quickly and positively is also key. Proactively planning with your team how best to respond in various scenarios will help ensure any negative experiences are transformed into positive ones, minimizing any potential harm to your reputation or brand image.

- *Be Present.* In today's digital age, it's tempting as an entrepreneur to work 24/7. However, prioritizing self-care in terms of mental, physical, and emotional well-being is not only beneficial for personal health but also for business success. Allowing yourself time away from work fosters creativity, which ultimately enhances long-term productivity—a win-win!

You Can Do It!

To achieve a successful transition into entrepreneurship, it is important to learn from mistakes and maintain focus on long-term goals. Utilizing resources like education, career counseling services, and networking opportunities can also be beneficial for those who have been laid off or face potential layoffs. With the right mindset, support system, and strategies in place, the possibilities are limitless! So don't let anything hinder your progress - take calculated risks while staying motivated; create efficient systems but stay present; build meaningful relationships but trust yourself – these are all key steps towards achieving success as an entrepreneur!

This story of resilience is a story of how one person—me—persevered despite the odds and stayed focus on their entrepreneurial dreams. It's a testament to the power of faith, inner strength, and the indomitable spirit that can rise above life's most daunting challenges. As I continue this transformative journey, ready to conquer the obstacles ahead and forge a path toward entrepreneurial fulfillment, I invite you to visit my website to explore real estate investing or tune into my podcast, *Bold Living Podcast*, for insights on wealth creation.

I pray that God will bless YOU with the vision to see yourself as he sees you and embrace the boundless potential within YOU. May this vision propel you toward the realization of your life's purpose, bringing fulfillment and success in all your endeavors.

Natoyah Grinnon, CEO of Apex Global Properties, specializes in mortgage notes, tax liens, and tax deeds. Her vision is to improve your financial well-being through long-term strategies and accessible investments. Serving on the REIA NYC legislative board, she offers insights on legal updates, while her Bold Living Podcast supports entrepreneurs and organizations in wealth building.

www.apexglobalproperties.com

AS IRON SHARPENS IRON

Peta-Gaye Jamieson

Black women entrepreneurs have long been trailblazers in business, despite the overwhelming odds against them. From Madame C.J Walker to Oprah Winfrey and beyond, these women have harnessed their creativity and resilience to create lasting legacies that are still celebrated today.

We often read about the challenges that these women faced in their lives and how they turned those challenges into successful businesses. These women are true warriors. Despite their success, the road to achieving success can still be especially difficult for Black women entrepreneurs due to systemic racism and ongoing issues of White male privilege in business.

According to the World Economic Forum, there has been a decrease in support for Black-founded startups, with a 45 percent drop in venture capital investments in 2022. This decline is especially alarming for Black women entrepreneurs, who typically receive a significantly lower portion of venture capital (VC) funding. In 2021, only 0.34 percent of all venture capital spending in the United States went to start-up founders who were Black women.[1]

---

[1] Lindiwe Matlali, "Black women lack access to VC funding. Here's what we can do.", March 27, 2023, World Economic Forum, https://www.weforum.org/agenda/2023/03/the-ebb-and-flow-of-vc-funding-how-to-support-black-women-in-business/.

Yes, the underrepresentation of Black women among female entrepreneurs in the United States is indeed a concerning statistic. Despite being part of a small minority, there has been an increase in visibility and platforms for these entrepreneurs to showcase their businesses and gain access to resources that can help them succeed.

As an immigrant from Jamaica, I experienced the same challenges and struggles that many of my fellow Black women entrepreneurs faced. When I first arrived in the United States, I believed the same thing that many immigrants do that getting an education would result in a well-paying job. However, after working in various positions over the years and never feeling like I was making what I was worth, I was inspired to pursue entrepreneurship.

Through my own journey as an entrepreneur, I learned that while it is possible to build a successful business on my own, it is much easier with support from other entrepreneurs who have similar experiences and understandings of what success looks like. This realization led me to creating The EZRA Group Inc., which is dedicated to providing resources for Black women entrepreneurs so they can reach their full potential.

In this chapter, I will discuss how the proverb "As iron sharpens iron, so one person sharpens another" (Proverbs 27:17) can be a practical principle for achieving success in modern-day business.

Let's discuss how we can improve the situation based on my experience.

Collaboration

Collaboration is key. Black women entrepreneurs must come together to support one another and share resources in order to make progress.

When Black women entrepreneurs collaborate, they can create mentorship programs, co-working spaces, and other entrepreneurial opportunities that will help them triumph over the challenges of systemic racism and White male privilege.

By working together and sharing ideas, resources, and experiences with one another, these courageous businesswomen can create a powerful network of successful female entrepreneurs who can serve as role models for future generations of Black women in business. This will also have the added benefit of creating opportunities for more diverse leadership within American businesses.

Collaboration can be seen throughout the Bible. The Bible contains many verses which emphasize the importance of collaboration with others in order to sharpen our skills and increase our effectiveness. In addition to Proverbs 27:17 quoted above, Ecclesiastes 4:9-10 expands on this idea, encouraging us to seek out help when we need it and to be willing to offer our own support. Proverbs 15:22 is another verse that speaks to the power of collaboration, emphasizing the importance of seeking counsel from others in order for plans to succeed. Romans 12:4-5 and 1 Corinthians 12:12 remind us that even though we are individuals, we are all part of a larger whole and that by working together, we can achieve more than if we worked alone.

Benefits of Collaboration

Collaboration has a range of advantages for both individuals and organizations. Let's look at some prominent examples:

Financial Gains

A company that collaborates with another business can increase sales and reduce costs through shared or combined resources. For example, two furniture manufacturers might partner together to pursue more lucrative contracts. With the combination of skills from each company, they can provide high-value services and goods that could not have been achieved by either one working independently.

Issa Rae is a successful Black female entrepreneur who achieved financial success and growth through collaborating with others across multiple industries. In 2018, Issa Rae Productions partnered with Warner Media to create the hit television series *Insecure* and various other projects. Through this partnership, Rae was able to expand her reach and increase her finances significantly. She also signed a multiyear deal with Netflix in 2020, which will allow her to develop new shows for streaming on the platform as well as produce additional content for HBO Max. Through these collaborations, Rae has been able to build an incredibly successful career as an actor, writer, producer, and businesswoman.[2]

Higher Productivity

In a collaborative environment, teams are able to access data with less friction and delays compared to working alone. When different departments are able to share real-time information through collaboration tools, this helps speed up operations and boost productivity within the company. This makes it much easier for employees or departments to find solutions to problems quickly without manual intervention.

For instance, Black female entrepreneurs living in different parts of the country can now work together on projects without having to physically meet. They can also bring in a range of specialists from different fields to help them in their venture without leaving the comfort of their homes. By taking advantage of these tools, they are more likely to succeed in their businesses

[2] Angelique Jackson, "Issa Rae Inks Eight-Figure Film and Television Deal With WarnerMedia,"
March 24, 2021, *Variety*, https://variety.com/2021/tv/news/issa-rae-hbo-max-warnermedia-film-television-deal-1234935944/.

than if they had to rely on traditional methods which take longer and cost more money.

Improved Employee Engagement and Well-Being

One of the key benefits of collaboration for Black women entrepreneurs is improved employee engagement and well-being. By working together, employees can build trust with one other and take ownership of their projects in order to reach their goals. This helps create a sense of unity and connection among team members that can lead to higher job satisfaction and improved engagement throughout the company.

Research has shown that workplace connectedness leads to positive work outcomes such as increased motivation, increased creativity and innovation, higher job satisfaction, lower levels of burnout, and better overall performance. This is especially important for Black women who are often underrepresented or overlooked in many workplaces.

When Black women collaborate, they also can benefit from collective wisdom as well as support when facing challenges or difficult situations. With a greater collective support system behind them, Black women entrepreneurs are more likely to have access to the resources they need to make progress in their businesses. This includes advice on managing finances, finding mentorships, networking opportunities and more.

Learning Opportunities

Collaboration also provides opportunities for learning and personal growth, which is especially beneficial to Black women entrepreneurs. Working with a team of diverse individuals who have different skill sets and backgrounds, helps to expand the knowledge base of everyone involved.

By collaborating and exchanging ideas, entrepreneurs can gain insight into new approaches to problem-solving they may not have thought of before. They can also benefit from constructive feedback that can help them become better business owners and leaders. This type of collaboration creates an environment in which each person can learn from other's experiences and use this to their advantage when taking on challenging tasks or developing new strategies.

Small Business Collaboration Benefits

Collaboration can also benefit small businesses in a number of ways. Working with others allows small business owners to access resources that they may not have had access to before, such as capital and technology. It also helps them reach new markets or customer bases which can lead to increased revenue.

When Black women entrepreneurs join forces and work together, it gives them more purchasing power and allows them to negotiate better deals on supplies, services, and products. This can allow them to keep their costs low while still having access to the resources they need in order to run their businesses.

One success story we can learn from is that of Patrice Banks, the owner of Girls Auto Clinic. Banks is a former engineer who decided to launch her own car repair shop that caters exclusively to women. By collaborating with other experts in the field, such as mechanics and auto parts suppliers, Banks was able to gain access to the resources she needed to ensure success for her business.[3]

Barriers to Collaboration

Black women entrepreneurs face numerous barriers when attempting to collaborate with one another. The lack of access to resources and capital can make it difficult for them to secure

---

[3] Wendy Solomon, "Patrice Banks: An Auto Clinic Where Girls Rule," December 9, 2016, Lehigh University website, https://www2.lehigh.edu/news/patrice-banks-an-auto-clinic-where-girls-rule.

funding or find the right partners. Additionally, systemic racism imposes its own unique challenges on Black female entrepreneurs, making it harder for them to succeed in their endeavors. Trust issues between team members can also present a major barrier, as people from different backgrounds and perspectives may clash if they don't feel respected or valued. To overcome this, successful teams need to create systems for feedback, conflict resolution, and decision-making that allow everyone's voice to be heard.

Competition mindset is another obstacle that Black women entrepreneurs have to tackle when attempting collaboration. The fear of being overlooked or not given the same opportunities can lead them to view potential partnerships as a competition rather than an opportunity for growth. This attitude can damage trust between team members and hinder communication, making it difficult for deals to move forward successfully. Furthermore, a lack of representation in many industries creates feelings of isolation among Black women entrepreneurs which further fuels the competitive mindset.

How Can We Be More Collaborative?

Although there may be obstacles, there are ways to overcome them. Here are some tips for Black female entrepreneurs to collaborate effectively.

Create the Environment

The first step is to create an environment where everyone involved in the collaboration feels comfortable sharing their ideas and experiences.

This means creating equal ground for all parties so each individual can contribute fully to the project. This is especially important for Black women, who may not feel as comfortable speaking up in a traditionally White-dominated space. Therefore, it's essential for all members of the team to be on the same page when it comes to collaboration and to ensure that everyone has an equal say in decisions that are made.

One method of achieving this is through establishing clear communication channels and creating an atmosphere of mutual respect between all participants. This can be done through holding regular meetings when everyone has the opportunity to express their ideas and opinions without fear of judgment or criticism. Regular check-ins should also be implemented throughout the collaboration process to make sure that everyone is still on track and that progress is being made.

It's also important to create a safe space where diversity and inclusion are embraced and encouraged. Allowing people from different backgrounds and experiences to share their unique perspectives can help challenge existing assumptions, broaden viewpoints, and create innovative solutions that weren't thought possible before. By embracing diversity, Black women entrepreneurs will have more support in growing their businesses than if they had to rely solely on their own resources or those of traditional institutions.

Define Goals

In order for collaboration to be successful, it's important to set clear goals and objectives for the project. This helps ensure that everyone is on the same page when it comes to what needs to be accomplished and how it should be done. It also allows teams to measure their progress throughout the process so they can make adjustments as needed in order to reach their targets.

It is also advisable to create a timeline so that participants know when tasks need to be completed by. Setting expectations early on ensures that everyone involved in the collaboration understands what is expected of them which makes it easier for them to work together efficiently.

For instance, when starting a business project, Black women entrepreneurs should decide what the end goal is and then break it down into smaller tasks. This will help to keep everyone organized and focused on the project instead of getting sidetracked.

Encourage Feedback, Problem-Solving Skills, and Shared Value

When collaborating on a project, it is essential to promote open dialogue among team members and encourage the sharing of feedback and ideas. This can be done through regular meetings when everyone has an opportunity to express their thoughts and opinions. By creating this kind of environment, companies can benefit from the different perspectives that each person brings to the table. This leads to more innovative solutions, and aids in fostering inclusivity.

In addition, encouraging team members to share valuable resources such as knowledge and tools can help increase efficiency as well as aid in skill development. For example, a female entrepreneur could access the experience and contacts of other collaborators that could help her progress in her business endeavors. It is also important for each individual involved to understand their contributions and value in order to keep morale high and maintain motivation levels throughout the process.

By facilitating an atmosphere of cooperation, effective problem-solving skills, creative solutions, and shared values are fostered. Through these approaches, businesses can stimulate growth while recognizing individual efforts and ensuring that everyone feels included within the project as a whole.

Celebrate Successes

Finally, it's important to celebrate successes and recognize the hard work of all participants. This helps to build morale within the team as well as create a sense of accomplishment that can be used to fuel further progress in the future.

Taking the time to acknowledge achievements, no matter how small, can help foster an environment where everyone feels appreciated for their efforts and encourages them to keep going even when faced with challenges. This type of recognition is especially beneficial to Black women entrepreneurs who may not always feel seen or heard in traditional business settings.

Collaboration is an important tool for Black women entrepreneurs to have in their arsenal, as it can provide access to resources and knowledge that may not be available otherwise. By creating a safe space where everyone feels respected and valued, setting clear goals with timelines, encouraging feedback and problem-solving skills, sharing value amongst team members, and celebrating successes along the way; collaboration can help ensure success for all involved. By providing guidance, inspiration, and support, my hope is that I can help Black women entrepreneurs to take their businesses to new heights. It is my dream that these individuals will become role models for future generations and create a brighter future for themselves and those that come after them.

Peta-Gaye Jamieson, founder of the EZRA Group Inc, developed The Architects of Your Business Foundation—a mobile platform that assists frustrated and overwhelmed Black and Brown first-time homebuyers, ages thirty-five to fifty-five, through creative financing strategies. It fosters collaboration, knowledge sharing, and support between users and service providers in a secure environment.

www.theezragroup.com

THE RESILIENT RETIREE: A RESILIENT JOURNEY

Velma A. Knights

You exhale deeply, and suddenly you realize you are closer to the next chapter of life: retirement. Though you may have been eagerly anticipating this moment, you find yourself lacking direction on how to proceed.

I can relate to what you are feeling. This was my situation at the end of 2019. Unfortunately, like other milestone moments in my life, no one had really prepared me for what was to come. Then in 2020, COVID-19 struck, making it necessary to think ahead and make diligent plans for an uncertain future.

You can attend all the classes, Zoom meetings, and webinars offered to those preparing for retirement. You can check the various websites and focus your attention on your future finances as is suggested, paying attention to inflation and how it might affect your future. This is all good advice and good practice. However, retirement is more than finances, and it was this aspect of retirement for which I was unprepared.

I have come across too many people who refuse to leave the workforce—not because they enjoy what they do, but because their main motivation is the desire to stay active and engaged. All too often, people cling to their jobs after retirement because they lack the vision of what life would be like without them. They're afraid they would have nothing to do and no one to associate with after retirement.

I myself may have subconsciously fallen into this category. I could have retired in 2005, but I enjoyed what I was doing and saw no need to leave. In January 2016, I announced my plans to retire, but my work was still enjoyable, so I stayed. Fast-forward to 2019—upheaval and drastic changes in the workplace forced me out of my comfort zone, and I decided it was finally time to go. But it wasn't until July 2021 that I stopped working altogether and crossed the finish line.

Unfortunately, the retirement finish line was not what I expected. I was single, had no children, and now that I had stopped going to work, I lost my professional community. Retirement can be a very emotional transition. It has been said that the two most vulnerable times in your life are the first year after your birth and the first twelve months after retirement.

After I stopped working, I started looking for my next endeavor. How could I live a resilient and ageless life with the time I had left? I started researching on the internet, reading blogs and articles on retirement and aging, especially those concerning baby boomers like myself. Most retirement advice covers finances. But the emotional and social aspects of retirement are often overlooked. My finances were okay, but what to pursue next was still up in the air. I certainly did not want to spend a vast amount of my life doing nothing. In doing research, I discovered that one in seven boomers is treated for depression at a higher rate than other generations of American adults.[4] And one of the causes for this depression is a lifestyle change such as retirement. Utilizing the information from my research, I knew I needed to find clarity. Finding clarity is no easy feat; it's much easier said than done. It

[4] Justin McCarthy, "Reports of Depression Treatment Highest Among Baby Boomers," January 30, 2015, Gallup, https://news.gallup.com/poll/181364/reports-depression-treatment-highest-among-baby-boomers.aspx.

takes a real dedication to self-reflection—to actively listen from within to achieve a clear vision of the life you want, and then to build a new community and relationships based on this discovery. I knew that in order to live an ageless and resilient life, I would need to think beyond the traditional idea of retirement and decide what kind of person I wanted to be and with whom I wanted to spend my time.

One of the first things I did was to join REIA NYC, and I considered starting a business. To help me on my journey, I enrolled in a sixteen-week Workshop in Business Opportunities (WIBO) class, which taught me about entrepreneurship and how to start my own business. Once I finished the course, I felt more equipped with knowledge about how to handle finances, build relationships with clients, and create effective marketing strategies for my business.

I then took it upon myself to join an organization called Momentum Education, which emphasizes shifting from a mentality of scarcity to one of abundance. The mission of this organization is centered around the belief that everyone matters and that together we can strive to create a win-win world. It was through this organization that I started to develop my new purpose for living outside work.

With my newfound confidence, I founded Resilient Empowered Ageless Living, LLC, a resource center designed specifically for individuals transitioning into retirement—a place where they can find support, guidance, and mentorship during this period of their lives. At REAL, our workshops are designed to equip individuals transitioning into retirement with the tools they need to lead resilient and fulfilled lives.

REAL takes a real approach to retirement and provides intentional resources aimed at guiding individuals through this stage. We understand that these individuals have worked hard for years and may now feel uncertain about how to use their newfound freedom. If we think about the way we entered adulthood, there were many resources that helped guide us to the path we are on today. The finish line is not the last day of employment, but rather the start of a new chapter. So why don't we show that same level of care and attention when we reach the end of this chapter?

At REAL, we focus on helping individuals embrace the retired life by fostering the development of skills such as mindfulness, healthy lifestyle habits, and financial planning. By providing resources, workshops, and a community for individuals to explore their post-retirement path, we help retirees find clarity, purpose, and fulfillment in this new chapter of life. This comprehensive approach to retirement can make a significant difference in people's lives as they navigate this transition and discover new opportunities. Through newsletters, blogs, apps, podcasts and forums, we help individuals tap into their passions, develop meaningful relationships with others, and create paths for ongoing learning and growth. We ignite mindful strategies that lead to peace and happiness. We share relevant news items affecting retirees, such as social security and Medicare. Articles by experts, recommended books, and activities are also included to assist individuals in mapping out their next steps. We also offer advice on how to make a successful transition from a career into entrepreneurship or another type of business venture. At REAL, we recognize that many retirees are dealing with complex emotions surrounding the end of their working lives, so our programs also focus on creating opportunities for social connection in order to promote healthy relationships and foster a sense of community among retirees. Overall, our mission is centered around helping people redefine themselves during this period of transition so they can live a resilient life full of meaning and joy no matter what their age. We believe that retirement can be an opportunity for reinvention and growth!

How You Can Lead a Resilient Life

Now that you understand how I was able to create a resilient life after retirement, here are some tips that can help you to do the same:

Acknowledge Your Age

Acknowledging your age can be difficult, especially when you are transitioning into retirement. But it is important to remember that aging does not mean the end of life; rather, it can be a time of growth and renewal. Acknowledging your age gives you access to wisdom and experience that can inform decisions and help you create meaningful change in your life.

One way to do this is by recognizing how far you've come since starting your career or leaving school. Reflecting on the milestones you've achieved in life can remind you of the skills and knowledge that have helped to get you this far. These are valuable resources that will come in handy as you move into your post-retirement years.

Focus on Self-Discovery

It is also beneficial to look at retirement as an opportunity for self-discovery. As well as leveraging the skills acquired throughout our lives, once we retire, we should explore new passions and interests which we may have never had the time or energy to pursue before. This could include discovering a new hobby, learning a foreign language, traveling, volunteering, or taking classes at a local college or university—all activities that can help build resilience and provide joy throughout retirement.

Being a friend to technology is also part of self-discovery. As we move into an age of digital transformation, understanding the power of technology is useful for learning new skills, expanding our network, and connecting with other people who share our interests.

Set New Goals

Being resilient is about more than just getting through a difficult time; it's also about setting new goals and creating the life you want after retirement. Defining what success looks like and creating a plan to achieve your goals is essential for leading a resilient life in retirement. There are many ways to determine what success looks like and then develop a plan that works best for you. To start, it's important to identify your individual strengths and weaknesses, as well as the values and interests that motivate you. This will help create an understanding of the areas of life you should focus on in order to meet your goals. Make sure you set realistic expectations for yourself so you don't become overwhelmed or discouraged if things don't go according to plan. Having someone who shares similar goals or interests can help keep you on track and provide much-needed support during difficult times. Additionally, it's useful to establish a routine daily activity that brings joy and fulfillment into your life, such as walking, yoga, or meditation, or even just having coffee with friends once a week.

Make Wellness a Priority

Wellness is not a luxury; it's a necessity. As we transition into retirement, it is important to remember that our well-being should be a priority. Wellness encompasses physical, mental, and emotional health, and all three are essential for living an ageless and resilient life. While it may be tempting to focus solely on financial stability during retirement, good physical and mental health can add years to your life. Physical wellness can help reduce the risk of chronic diseases such as heart disease and diabetes that can have serious implications for post-retirement individuals.

Mental wellness is also key in helping retirees stay engaged and purposeful throughout their later years. Research has found that individuals who remain mentally active throughout their retirement experience fewer symptoms of depression than those who do not stay connected with their communities or pursue meaningful activities. Engaging in intellectual pursuits such as taking classes or joining book clubs can go a long way in promoting positive mental health once you're retired.

Emotional well-being is also vital for retirees seeking to lead healthy lives during this new phase of life; without feeling safe and secure within their environment, many retirees struggle to find joy amid the uncertainty of this period of transition. Developing meaningful relationships with family members, friends, and mentors provides comfort during times of change while fostering camaraderie and connection to others within the community.

At REAL, we acknowledge that prioritizing wellness is crucial for all retirees. By taking action to maintain physical, mental, and emotional health, you can lead an ageless life full of resilience, even as you experience the changes that come with aging.

My journey to create a resilient life after retirement has been an eye-opening experience, and I am proud of how far I have come. I am embracing this newfound freedom and flexibility. As I've gotten to know myself again as an individual and begun to see everything that is in store for me, I want others to do the same. I hope the tips outlined here will help you find your own path, as you discover new things and set new goals. If you are embarking on this new phase of life and seeking guidance, I encourage you to start exploring today and begin the journey to becoming a resilient, empowered, and ageless retiree.

Velma A. Knights is an inspirational figure and the founder and owner of Resilient Empowered Ageless Living, LLC (R.E.A.L.). She is dedicated to redefining the concept of ageless living for retirees and creating a community that embraces resilience and empowerment.

www.realagelessliving.com

THE POWER OF SELF-IDENTITY

Phoenixx Martin

Do you ever feel like you're not living up to your full potential or are overwhelmed by the demands of everyday life? Are you constantly trying to fit in or keep up with "the Joneses"? If you've answered yes to any of these questions, you're not alone. In fact, millions of people are dealing with these same struggles. Many of us have asked ourselves, "Who am I?" and "What sets me apart from everyone else?"

Just a few years ago, I felt the same way. The misconceptions I developed over the years were having a negative impact on my ability to move forward with my life. I was ready for a change in my life, but I had absolutely no idea how to start. All I knew was that a change needed to happen— and quick!

For a while, I struggled to express my true identity and never felt confident or comfortable in my own skin. This led to feelings of insecurity, low self-esteem, and lack of direction. I was desperate for a real solution in order to turn my life around. What I discovered completely changed my life! I learned that if you want to take control of your life and reach your full potential, you need to be aware of how your identity affects you.

In this chapter, I'm going to share the best strategies I've found to help you gain a better understanding of who you are and what you're capable of achieving. Let's go!

What Is Identity?

Identity is a complex and ever-evolving concept. It is the foundation of how we interact with the world around us and how others perceive us. It consists of many components, such as our culture, beliefs, values, lifestyle, and physical appearance. Each component contributes to our overall identity, creating a unique sense of self.

Our identity is constantly in flux. Our experiences, relationships, environment, and even personal preferences can shape our identity. This can lead to a deep understanding of ourselves and how we view the world. Our identity is also impacted by larger societal forces such as education systems, cultural norms, or economic systems. All these factors contribute to how we identify and can either strengthen or weaken our sense of self.

It is important to understand that identity is not fixed or absolute. Rather, it is ever-changing and can be influenced by our actions or by the actions of those around us. A complex combination of many elements come together to form our unique and personal identity. By understanding our identity, we can better navigate the world around us and make informed decisions about our future.

My own identity was shaped by my childhood experiences, which were not all positive. The trauma of child molestation greatly changed my self-esteem and perspective of the world and everything in it and everyone around me. I struggled to make sense of what had happened to me and how to cope with the intense emotions it stirred up. This trauma was compounded with the diagnosis of autism spectrum disorder when I was eight years old.

How Identity Is Formed

Our identity is one of the most important aspects of our lives. It helps us to define who we are and can shape our experiences, interactions, and beliefs. But how is identity formed?

Our family is one of the most influential factors in forming our identity. Our family gives us a sense of belonging and establishes values, expectations, and behaviors that shape our outlook on life. The culture we grow up in can also have a big influence on how we view ourselves and the world around us.

Our environment, including the physical and social surroundings we grow up in, can affect our identity as well. Religion can also play a role in developing our identity, as it provides us with an understanding of life's purpose and meaning.

Because, at an early age, I was the victim of an attack at the hands of a member of my family, this experience deeply influenced my identity. Some family members turned against me and even tried to get me to change the narrative of what I "thought" happened when I finally mustered up the courage to come forward with what was going on, and this experience had an impact on my sense of self. The issue was swept under the rug, and my attacker was never held accountable for what he had done to me. It made me feel dirty and ashamed, and I struggled to trust people. I felt silenced and ignored, which caused me to develop a very shy and timid personality. Later, when I was diagnosed with autism, this further impacted my sense of self. I felt like I was different from others and didn't fit in.

As I grew older, I faced various other challenges such as bipolar depression and anxiety, chronic pain disorder, and epilepsy. I also had to undergo a double mastectomy due to discovering I had the BRCA1 gene, which put me at a higher risk of developing breast cancer. All these experiences shaped my identity and made me who I am today.

Personal Identity versus Sense of Self

Personal identity and sense of self are two constructs that are often used interchangeably but have distinct differences. *Personal identity* refers to the unique attributes, characteristics, and traits that define an individual's identity, including their values, beliefs, personality, and experiences. *Sense of self*, on the other hand, refers to an individual's subjective perception of themselves, including their self-concept, self-esteem, and self-image.

In my case, my personal identity was shaped by the hardships I faced and the coping strategies I used to overcome them. My experiences with child molestation, autism spectrum disorder, and various illnesses contributed to my identity and shaped my values and beliefs. However, my sense of self was affected by these experiences, as I struggled with self-esteem and body dysmorphia.

Factors That Influence Self-Identity:

- **Family** plays a significant role in shaping an individual's self-identity. Parents, siblings, and other family members can shape an individual's beliefs, values, and worldview.

- **The culture and society** in which an individual grows up influence their self-identity. Social norms, customs, and traditions shape an individual's beliefs, values, and behaviors.

- An individual's **gender identity and sexual orientation** also shapes their self-identity. Society's expectations and stereotypes regarding gender and sexuality influence an individual's self-identity too.

- **Education** plays a crucial role in shaping an individual's self-identity. Education helps individuals develop their values, beliefs, and critical thinking skills.

- **Life experiences** such as trauma, success, failure, and personal achievements shape an individual's self-identity.

- **Media and technology** can influence an individual's self-identity. Social media platforms, for example, can shape an individual's perception of themselves and others.

- **Personal relationships** influence an individual's self-identity. Relationships with friends, romantic partners, and family members all shape an individual's beliefs, values, and personality traits.

Our sense of self is what makes us who we are. It's the combination of our thoughts, feelings, and beliefs that shapes our identity. However, it's not always easy to maintain a strong sense of self, especially in the face of challenges and adversity. Here are a few tips to help strengthen your sense of self:

- **Identify your values and beliefs:** Consider the things you value and why you value them. What are your top priorities? What are your stances on the most essential issues? Having these written down will allow you to quickly refer to them anytime you need guidance.

- **Practice self-care:** Taking care of yourself is an important aspect of building a strong sense of self. This can include adopting a healthier lifestyle by choosing better food options, getting enough sleep, and exercising regularly. By prioritizing your physical and mental health, you'll feel better about yourself and more confident in your abilities.

- **Challenge negative self-talk:** Negative self-talk can undermine your sense of self and hold you back from reaching your full potential. When you catch yourself engaging in negative self-talk, challenge those thoughts by questioning their validity. Ask yourself if these are based on fact or simply your insecurities.

- **Set goals and work toward them:** Setting goals gives you a sense of purpose and direction, which can help strengthen your sense of self. Make sure your goals are realistic and achievable, and then break them down into smaller, manageable steps. Maintain your drive by constantly rewarding and acknowledging your progress.

- **Connect with others:** Building strong relationships with others can help you feel more connected and grounded, which in turn strengthens your sense of self. Seek out supportive friends and family members and make an effort to spend time with them regularly.

- **Use mindfulness in your daily life:** Meditating on the present moment without passing judgment on it is what mindfulness is all about. By practicing mindfulness, you can learn to tune out distractions and focus on what's important, and this will help you to build a stronger sense of self.

Know Your Core Values

In our journey of self-discovery, uncovering our core values is one of the most important things we can do. Our values are the beliefs and principles that guide our actions and decisions and ultimately shape the course of our lives. Let's look at how our values influence our thoughts and behaviors and discover ways we can use them to overcome obstacles and live a fulfilling life.

Living a values-driven life means aligning your actions and decisions with your values. A values-driven life is fulfilling, purposeful, and authentic. When you embrace your values, you become more self-aware, more confident, and more empowered. Take some time to reflect on what is important to you. Write down your values and prioritize them. For example, look back at your life and think about the moments that have shaped you. What were the experiences that made you feel happy, fulfilled, and proud? What were the experiences that made you feel unhappy, unfulfilled, and disappointed? These moments can provide valuable insight into your core values. Ask yourself what you want to stand for and what kind of person you want to be. Then, clarify your purpose and set specific, measurable, achievable, relevant, and time-bound (SMART) goals that align with your values and purpose.

Tips for Personal Growth

Personal growth is an essential aspect of our identity, and it is essential to embrace this process to become the best version of ourselves. The following tips have helped me grow and develop as an individual:

Adopt a healthier lifestyle by eating better: Eating healthier is one of the best steps you can take toward achieving personal growth. By making smart and mindful choices when it comes to food, you can easily make positive changes to your physical, mental, and emotional health. Healthy eating has helped me feel more energized and focused, which has improved my overall well-being.

Start by setting realistic goals you can gradually build upon. You may want to focus on limiting your sugar intake, eating more fruits and vegetables, or cutting down on processed foods. Make sure to also stay hydrated and drink plenty of water throughout the day. Taking small steps toward healthier eating can help you become more energized and motivated to strive toward personal growth.

Redirect negative thoughts: When I find myself thinking negatively, I try to replace those thoughts with positive affirmations. Negative thoughts can often be overwhelming and difficult to process. However, it's important to recognize that these thoughts are not always true—and *you* have the power to control them. To redirect negative thoughts, start by identifying them when they come up.

If you find yourself worrying about something in the future, take a step back and bring yourself back to the present moment.

Remind yourself that you don't know what will happen and that worrying won't make anything better. Reframe the negative thought as an opportunity for growth and focus on what you can do to improve the situation.

Exercise regularly: Exercise has been a great way for me to manage my anxiety and depression. Not only it can improve your physical health, but it can also be beneficial to your mental health as well. Studies show that exercise can help increase self-esteem and self-confidence, allowing you to feel better about yourself.

When it comes to exercising for self-identity, there are several different things you can do. You can try aerobic exercises such as running or swimming, or you can focus on strengthening exercises such as weightlifting or yoga.

Meditate and pray: Finding time for prayer and meditation is a powerful tool to help you focus on your self-identity. Meditation and prayer help you to clear your mind, allowing you to better process thoughts and feelings about yourself. Meditation and prayer also help to relieve stress and anxiety, allowing for a calmer and clearer state of mind.

When meditating and praying, focus on positive affirmations. Make sure you take the time to listen to yourself and believe what you are saying. Remind yourself of the good qualities you possess and allow yourself to relax at the moment. Meditation and prayer have helped me to stay centered and focused on my goals.

Have a weekly check-in with yourself: Recognize your accomplishments and give yourself the same grace you give to others. Doing this regularly has helped me develop a positive mindset and recognize my strengths.

Taking time for yourself is a great way to practice self-care and identify areas of growth. Setting aside time each week for a check-in with yourself is beneficial to your overall well-being. This check-in should involve assessing how you're feeling emotionally, mentally, and physically and allow you to take stock of any changes that have occurred since the last check-in.

The purpose of the weekly check-in is to provide a safe space for you to recognize any changes in your mood, behavior, or outlook. Additionally, it's important to reflect on any areas of your life that you'd like to work on, such as becoming more organized or reducing stress.

Create a safe space for yourself: It's important to separate yourself from the pressures of the outside world, reflect on your thoughts and feelings, and connect with your true sense of self. Creating a safe space for yourself will help you feel more connected to yourself and better prepared to face the challenges life throws your way.

The first step in creating a safe space for yourself is to define what that means for you. Do you want it to be a physical space, like a bedroom or office? Or do you want to create an emotional and mental sanctuary in your mind? Once you've identified the type of safe space you need, make sure you have everything you need to make it comfortable and calming.

Create a safe space for others: Do this by allowing others to be themselves and find ways to celebrate their authenticity. Doing this has helped me connect with others on a deeper level and build meaningful relationships.

It's also important to refrain from making assumptions about other people. Try not to jump to conclusions based on their physical characteristics, cultural backgrounds, or any other factors that could lead to stereotypes or discrimination. Instead, approach everyone with an open mind and get to know them on a personal level.

My experiences and journey toward understanding self-identity led me to become a life coach. I now help people overcome their struggles by guiding them to discover their true identities. My coaching sessions focus on self-love and acceptance, empowering my students or readers to create a life they love.

As a non-binary person of color, **Phoenixx Martin** is a New York native residing in Philadelphia, Pennsylvania. A Certified Empowerment and Confidence Life Coach and human rights, animal rights, and LGBTQIA+ rights advocate, Phoenixx guides clients in identifying their inner strengths and conquering the perceived barriers that hold them back.

www.phoenixxmartin.com

A BUSINESS BUILT TO BLESS: FINDING PASSION AND PURPOSE IN CHAOS

Dr. Teresa R. Martin

To understand how you can use your business to bless others, you must first hear my story. For as long as I could remember, I've always wanted to be an attorney. The thought just came to my head, and I always kept my eyes on that goal. In high school, I became a teen mother and swore that I would not become a statistic. I swore to do right by my child and myself by finishing high school and going on to college. I admit, it wasn't easy. Life isn't always smooth sailing. Some people have it hard, others don't—that's just the reality. I stayed focused, kept my head in the books, and did what I had to do no matter how hard, exhausting, and challenging it seemed.

I focused on becoming an incredible mother and graduating high school, and I then went on to achieve my associate's, bachelor's, and juris doctorate degrees. My career eventually took me to the New York City Law Department, where I worked on litigation cases for the NYPD. Everything was working out. My children were well-provided for. I had a lovely, custom-built home in the Poconos. But when 9/11 hit, my world was turned upside down. My office was one block from the attack. Suddenly nothing I owned was truly permanent—not my career, my home, or my impressive financial portfolio. I was left jobless for months, and my home went into foreclosure despite numerous pleas to the lender. I was on the verge of bankruptcy and facing complete financial ruin. *How could this have happened to me?* I wondered over and over.

I did everything that I could to embrace my inner strength through my spiritual beliefs. I heard a still, small voice say, "Just trust in me, trust in me with all your heart. Do not depend on your own understanding." Something inside of me told me to keep my head up and fight, to believe that things would get better. Eventually, the bankruptcy case was dismissed, and I was allowed to sell my home and even gained a significant profit from that situation. Those humbling experiences were my wake-up call. I learned that when things may seem dismal, nothing is truly lost, and there is always a way out. Every path needs to be clarified.

I realized that my mission was to travel the road of entrepreneurship and create something tangible (and permanent) for myself—something that couldn't be taken away from me, no matter what. I became a real estate, bankruptcy, and foreclosure defense attorney so I could help other women rebuild their wealth with real estate and gain financial freedom. I learned that you cannot have a testimony without a test. I went from losing one home to having a large real estate portfolio, and now I help others to achieve their dreams of home ownership, financial security, and business ownership. I help people to build generational wealth instead of generational poverty. Real estate and financial empowerment are now my ministry, and I love it.

What does it take to start a business? Playing this entrepreneurial game requires grit, drive, and a hustler's mindset. Grit will help you in the face of any adversity. There are highs and lows in life, and how you take those low moments will determine how far you go in your business. Being a business owner isn't easy because there is no consistent paycheck at the end of the week. There is no time to slack off. Your paycheck is what you put into it, which can be a scary reality if you've become comfortable with the structure and security that a nine-to-five provides. When you don't have all the answers, when nothing seems to be working, and when you haven't got any sales, grit will help you to keep pushing through until you get that first sale. Grit will be your best friend to keep you focused and rolling with the punches.

Why do you wake up every single morning and go to work? Everyone has a reason behind *why* they do things in life. It's time for you to get honest with your why. Why do you want to start a business? Why do you want to go down this path? There are positives and negatives in everything in this life. Figure out your why and stick to it. Let your why be the driving focus to keep pushing forward.

A hustler mentality will take you far. When you are first starting your business, there are no breaks and no cutbacks. Deploy the mindset of a *go-getter*; if you want it bad enough and the stakes are high enough, run after it. Get out there and make connections. Develop a thick skin when it comes to other people's critiques. Learn from others, but take things with a grain of salt, drop all excuses, and carry yourself with confidence. If you don't feel confident, then act as if you are confident until it's second nature.

Look into new ways to find new clients. Look for ideas to enhance and improve your business. You must sacrifice time spent with family. You'll have to cut back on entertainment funds to build your business. It may seem like a daunting road. I'm giving you the ugly truth—the not-so-glamorous side of what it will take to become a business owner. The truth is, in the beginning, you must think like a hustler—you must be a hustler!

Challenge yourself every single day to do something impactful, something that moves the needle for your business. The best thing you can do is get enthusiastic about your business and promote yourself everywhere. Connect and network with other people—

actively put yourself out there. When you dedicate yourself to your business daily, you will develop more confidence and become adept at meeting and overcoming challenges.

If you want to venture down this road, you'll need to deploy grit and stoicism. Shift your thinking and know that you are blessed as a human on this earth. You are capable of so much more simply by existing. All the power you have lies within you. Remember that becoming an entrepreneur is one of the best decisions a person can make.

Steps to Attainment

The overall goal as an entrepreneur is to create a successful, thriving business. But how do you get there? Follow these steps:

1. **Brainstorm and set attainable, realistic, measurable goals that can be carried out in a practical time frame.** Setting goals keeps you motivated and focused on what truly matters—your why. Start each day with an overall objective of what needs to be accomplished—for example, creating social media platforms to increase online traffic to your business organically.

2. **Get clear on the steps you'll need to take to reach those goals.** It could be something as simple as launching a website for your business. Let's say that you want to launch by the end of the month. Spend that month researching the market, looking at competitors, and finding a way to bring what is missing to the market. Commit to your business in small increments daily, taking on something different and new. This will help you to feel less overwhelmed. This method will help make the learning curve run more smoothly for you.

3. **Set deadlines and stick to them.** Have an end goal for your business at the end of each month to get the ball rolling. You

want to make sure you're doing everything properly and efficiently. The more time you spend fine-tuning details within your company, the more your hard work and efforts will pay off.

A Business That Blesses

You can bless others in business by your service. Blessers in business are entrepreneurs that want to do more than simply make a profit—they want to make a difference, too. Whether you're serving your clients as a virtual assistant or selling digital products and memberships, you can practice radical giving.

You can bless others in business by your dedicated focus. That's because those who want to bless others know who they want to serve. They have a target flock in mind that they're excited about and are passionate about serving them.

If your intentions are authentic and genuine, money will follow. Sometimes, giving back can be as easy as creating a list of things you already know how to do and then using what you know to teach, encourage, and assist others when they need help. In my case, I used my passion for law to become a real estate, bankruptcy, and foreclosure defense attorney with a special focus in wealth building management in real estate.

You can turn your passions, however small, into a business. For example, you might be passionate about supplies for organizational purposes. You work as an administrative assistant/ receptionist at a dental office, where you're great at keeping track of different priorities and deadlines. In college, you excelled at staying organized, took clear, concise notes, and always completed assignments on time. Well, you can sell those skills and services to others. You can create a business around teaching people to be organized, which blesses them by helping to make their lives better.

The most important thing is the value you bring to the table. How are you helping people? Are your products and services practical and valuable? If you treat your customers respectfully and show them kindness and professionalism, you're already off to a great start with excellent customer retention.

Don't Operate from a Place of Lack or Selfishness

When you believe that there is a limit to the money or goodness available, you can approach every situation with a belief that you must hoard things. You have to hold tightly to your money, your time, and your gifts.

The most common excuse is that the market is saturated. People often think that just because that business idea has already been done, you cannot succeed in that business. This is a lie. You can be successful in an industry that tens of thousands are profiting from. The difference is *you*. This world has not been blessed before with you and your creativity. Bless the market with your individuality and your uniqueness.

And don't think that just because you're helping others, that is taking away from you.

It's easy to think that because other people are awesome, you can't be awesome, too. That's because most people imagine the world as a small stage where only a few, truly gifted entrepreneurs can show off their talents.

But the stage is big enough to support everyone. This world is full of blessings. In fact, your product or service could be exactly what someone else needs. Helping others will only send good energy your way and give you a good reputation. More people will want to work with you, leading to more connections and earnings. There is no limit!

Setting boundaries is another way to stay blessed and faithful to your business. Don't be tempted to take on every client or project that comes your way for fear that if you don't, you might lose out on money or experience. This mindset keeps you from doing your best work. Instead, if a client or project doesn't resonate with you, say no. This opens up room in your business for clients and projects that you are truly passionate about.

The Value-Add in Business

Bless others and your business by adding value. This goes both ways. First, you'll get a return on your investment. When your business has a widespread reputation, more people will come, generating more sales for you or more traffic to your store, and more relationships and connections will be established.

Regardless of the business model or industry, develop a reputation for offering trustworthy, quality products or services, and people will always come back wanting more. It makes sense to invest in value and create a unique, tailored business for the people you are committed to serve. The more you put value into your business, the more people will want to engage with you.

Don't Let Pride Block the Blessing

When it comes to starting a new business, there's probably a lot you don't know. Sure, you might be skilled in a particular area, such as writing or graphic design. But do you know how to do your own bookkeeping? Are you familiar with your local business permit laws? Do you know how to protect your business with the right insurance?

A new business can be a humbling experience. Often, entrepreneurs jump in excitedly only to realize they don't know enough about running a business.

If you've hit this snag, don't let your pride get in the way. This is a wonderful time to seek wisdom and discernment. Connect with people who can help you achieve your goals. Maybe this means hiring a business coach or a lawyer who specializes in LLC formation.

Don't be afraid to reach out and get others involved. Be bold and converse with people who have done it before. A business can grow by leaps and bounds when you invite community into it!

It's All About Your Mindset

Your background, level of education, and economic status do not matter. It is all about mindset and what you do with your existing resources. Whether you are a business owner or have a part-time job, put some money away each time you get paid from your business. You have options, and there are solutions that can help get you out of your situation. If you do not own a business, you can still get a blessing from this chapter and learn from my experience.

My journey toward owning my own business started when I became a lawyer. I was passionate about law, but I didn't enjoy the reality of being a lawyer, the long hours, and the not-so-flexible schedule over time. It took a drastic, life-changing event that caused me to rethink everything. I decided to try something new by focusing more on the legal side of real estate. I homed in on something I was passionate about, and this is where my business journey began.

I coach from a place of firsthand knowledge of both struggles and successes. I have weathered financial ruin and job loss after 9/11 and investment losses after the mortgage crisis of 2008, both times coming out stronger and more resilient than before and eager to share my hard-earned expertise with other women in business. After the pandemic, I feel uniquely positioned to help women business owners pivot and build an unshakeable business in any economy.

Whatever the reason you started or are thinking about starting a business, remember that the biggest thing you can do as an entrepreneur is to bless others through your experiences and passion. Knowledge is a blessing, and owning a business is power. Create your business and bless others with your skills, abilities, and resources!

Dr. Teresa R. Martin, Esq.—"Dr. T"—is an accomplished attorney for women real estate entrepreneurs. With decades of experience as a consultant and entrepreneur in real estate investments, legal advising, and small businesses, she offers specialized consulting services that help female owners reach their goals with maximum efficiency.

www.drteresamartin.com

CREDIT CHANGES EVERYTHING: THE CLIMB FROM IGNORANCE

William Moore

The Journey Begins

In my early adult life, between 1994 and 2003—a ten-year period—I had my first exposure to credit, and this would have an ongoing impact on my life.

1994. Like most young guys, I wanted to purchase a car right after college, but despite having a job that paid well, I did not have a strong credit history. So I did what most people in my circumstance would have done: I asked my mother to co-sign on the loan. I promised to pay back the loan on time and maintain a stable employment with a modest cost of living. When my mother was a teenager, her credit was bad, but she eventually rebuilt it to be excellent.

My mother certainly found it difficult to reject me, but she didn't agree to co-sign. Instead, she said, "If you really want this car, you will find a way." Despite my disappointment, I took her advice and managed to find a solution. It was a bad idea, however. I visited a bad-credit dealership with exorbitant interest rates and expensive monthly payments. They eventually recognized that all I wanted was a car. I paid $550 per month, or $1,250 in today's dollars, in 1994 to purchase a used 1990 automobile at 22 percent interest. My capacity to invest, pursue my education, obtain a credit card, or purchase a home was hampered by the cost of getting that car.

1998. 1998 was the year I made the decision to be married. In addition to the daughter I had from a prior relationship, my fiancée had two children from her first marriage. I immediately recognized that I needed a home for my growing family, but I had no idea how to go about doing so. I'd only ever rented apartments since I was a Brooklyn kid. Just like the automobile, I was unprepared. My fiancée and I explained our search criteria to the realtor, who then pulled out three binders with the labels *Brooklyn*, *Queens*, and *Other*. The agent checked our credit reports, then removed the Brooklyn and Queens binder and opened the binder labeled *Other*. I ought to have seen how upset my fiancée was when they checked our credit. Since my fiancée's credit was poor and my scores were "fair," I would be the one getting the loan. The results showed that I was reasonable.

With my fair credit history, a new Staten Island construction was our only option. Staten Island seemed so far away, even though it was just across the Verrazano Bridge. I accepted the house despite the poor terms since I didn't have many other options. Consequently, predatory lending harmed a lot of people of color, including us. Although it was too expensive, I still bought the house.

2003. Fast-forward a few years. I'm married, with a new family and a mortgage. The timing was ideal because I qualified for a fast-tracked promotion within the New York Army National Guard, where my unit would be assisting in war efforts abroad. The promotion required managing government assets, so one's credit history was a big consideration.

I was overextended by my debts, including my mortgage, and my fair credit now was poor. I received an anonymous rejection without explanation. Fortunately, a friend in personnel informed me that the main reason I was rejected was because of my credit score. My bad credit was a red flag despite the fact that I was overqualified and well-liked in my battalion. I resigned my commission from the National Guard six months after being turned down and started looking into other options.

The Climb from Ignorance

Years after leaving the National Guard, I started working in direct sales to supplement my income. Early on, my mentor was instrumental in my success. One day he asked me to drive to Connecticut to meet a speaker. Prior to doing business with the speaker, my mentor wanted my opinion. The details of the event altered my life and inspired me to start my business. This speaker represented a credit-improvement business. The three-hour seminar provided context for the previous ten years that influenced my life. My errors and their consequences made sense. I discovered the reasons why my credit was bad and that I wasn't to blame. I learned that I could raise both my status and my financial prospects. Finally, I received a recovery road map.

Sadly, my marriage didn't work out, and I left our home in late 2007. The world had changed during the time we were married, and the nation was on the verge of financial collapse. There were few options available, and there was no time to build credit. After my divorce, I struggled with depression, overwhelming debt, poor credit, and poor health. There was only one way to go from where I was, and that was up, so I started working.

The Path to Recovery

I chose to engage with a financial education services organization with the help of my mentor, and I soaked up all the information they had about the credit business. I became more knowledgeable about the credit industry and realized there was a connection between my credit and my finances. Because of my bad credit,

I had to pay more in interest and fees, which left me with less money in my pocket overall. I discovered that although much of the information on my credit report that was classified as negative was inaccurate, it still had an unfavorable effect on my scores. I made the decision that going "old school" was the only way for me to take charge of my finances.

In favor of a simple notepad and a pen, I said to heck with elaborate Excel spreadsheets. I recorded all my outgoing costs and compared them to my payroll period. I spoke with my creditors and established payment plans. I promised myself that I would never pay a bill after the due date again. Thanks to my direct sales business, I had the good fortune to generate additional cash, which I put to good use. My credit card companies received biweekly direct payments that I set up. I worked my direct sales business as part-time side hustle, which paid more than my full-time employment, and I used the extra money to pay off my debt.

I worked twelve to fifteen-hour days during those years. Day job until 5:30 p.m., sales meeting at 7:00 p.m., home at 10:30 p.m., computer at 11:30 p.m., and in bed by 1:00 a.m. Since my daughter resided with her mother in a different area of town, I had little time to spend with her due to my busy schedule. My daughter was my biggest supporter when I joined direct sales and left the army, so I made her a promise: "Even though I'm not as present, I'm investing this time to earn the money so when the time comes for you to go to college, you'll be able to go anyplace you want." She agreed.

In order to change my attitude toward my bills, I had to set a very strong "why" as a goal: to send my daughter to college. As a result, I started to see results. I've learned from working in the direct sales industry that establishing trusting relationships is essential for success. Even though it took a lot of work, it can pay off handsomely if done right. I learned so much from my mentor, who was among the greatest in the business. The outcome? I finally paid off all my debts eighteen months after I made that pledge to my daughter. I learned about the relationship between my finances and credit. I was able to pay off all my credit cards thanks to the money I made from my direct sales business, and as a result, I received a $2,300 overpayment check along with the remark, "Stop sending us money—your accounts are paid in full." I also started getting letters from Experian, Equifax, and TransUnion praising me for enhancing my credit profile. I improved my scores from 515 to 720 between 2007 and 2010. When my daughter was ready to go to college in 2010, I stayed true to my word. "Daddy did his part; it's up to you now," I told her after paying the first two years' tuition at the school's finance office.

The Score Tells—The Report Sells

In 1989 and 2006, FICO and Vantage rating systems standardized the modern credit industry, which began in 3500 BC. Understanding my credit score helped me improve it. For American consumers, it's important to understand how scores are determined:

- Payment history for loans and credit cards: 35 percent
- Credit usage: no more than 30 percent of your available credit
- Length of credit history: 15 percent
- Newly reported credit by credit bureaus: 10 percent
- Credit mix: 10 percent, including loans for cars, houses, and credit cards

Understanding how credit impacts your daily life is essential in an environment where inflation can vary every five to ten years. Your wallet will be impacted because higher credit scores equate to lower interest rates. Sadly, the average American consumer never associates credit with their daily spending, so they are fearful of living paycheck to paycheck. Learn how to master the five ways above to master your credit, and then you can teach others.

I have come a long way in understanding the importance of credit. It wasn't until I experienced the negative consequences of poor credit that I realized just how crucial it is to maintain a healthy credit score and report. In my journey, I transitioned from someone who neglected their credit to someone who now helps others understand and improve their credit scores.

I was able to understand my credit score and credit report because of my "real-life" education. I learned how to challenge inaccurate information on my report, and I learned the actions to take to raise my credit score, such as paying bills on time and paying off debt. I started to observe improvements in my life at the same time as my credit score started to rise. I was successful in getting a low-interest automobile loan and went on to make real estate investments. Aside from that, when my credit score rose, more opportunities became available to me.

Birth of a Business

I also learned the value of networking, and that's how I met Teresa, the love of my life. A prosperous entrepreneur, my wife counseled me against becoming a top seller and instead encouraged me to launch my own company. I managed to do it despite my anxiety. I reasoned that the person who had already gone through it could instruct others on how to escape financial hardship and repair their credit. I took the risk and established William D. Moore Consulting, Inc.

I was motivated by my experience to educate others on the value of credit and on how to raise their scores. I became a credit counselor and started coaching individuals and families on managing their credit. I've seen firsthand the way a low credit score can negatively impact someone's life, and I am passionate about helping others avoid the same mistakes I made.

In my role as a credit coach, I first instruct my clients on the fundamentals of credit, such as credit reports, credit scores, and how they are determined. I assist them in understanding the various aspects of their credit score, including payment history, credit use, and length of credit history. I give them additional information on how to access their credit reports and challenge any inaccurate information they may discover.

Together, we build a strategy to raise their credit scores once they comprehend the fundamentals of credit. This could entail setting up a spending plan, paying off debt, or settling outstanding debts through negotiation. I also offer advice on how to use credit cards properly and make payments on time.

When a client has a negative item on their credit report, such as a collection or a payment that was past due, I work with them to dispute the item and have it removed from their report. Although it may take some time, doing this will greatly raise their credit score; therefore, the effort is well worth it.

The improvement of my clients' life is my primary objective as a credit coach; it's not only improving their credit scores. A stronger credit score is the beginning, though; it can lead to better job opportunities, lower interest rates on loans and credit cards, and even better insurance rates. It can also reduce stress and anxiety related to financial struggles and help individuals and families achieve their goals and dreams.

My personal transformation from someone who ignored their credit to someone who assists others in improving their credit has been a life-changing process. I've seen firsthand how crucial credit is to our daily lives and how it can affect everything from getting loans to having a job. I'm passionate about educating people about improving their credit scores so they can enhance their lives and pursue their financial objectives. Regardless of their financial circumstances or past transgressions, I think everyone deserves the chance to build credit and achieve financial security.

It's never too late to start raising your credit score, and I strongly advise anyone having credit issues to get assistance from a credit coach or counselor. The world of credit can be difficult to understand, but with the correct support and advice, you can manage it and improve both your life and your credit score.

I provide credit education courses and seminars in addition to working with one-on-one clients. To increase financial literacy and assist people in making credit-related decisions that are well-informed, I think education is the key. I want to assist more real estate investors and entrepreneurs to avoid the perils of having bad credit and attain financial stability by educating them about the significance of credit.

Final Thoughts

You must understand that the way you manage each of the aforementioned elements will determine how every creditor views you. Your credit score may increase or decrease as a result of this knowledge. Be specific. The two biggest factors are payment history and amounts owed. That's how you'll be judged.

To recover financially, you must:

- Have a strong "why."
- Eliminate embarrassment, shame, and any other emotion from the equation; creditors don't care.
- Examine your income.
- Examine your expenses.
- Identify the sacrifices you need to make.
- Identify the finish line; set a goal and go for it.

Credit is more than just a number. It is an essential element of our lives that affects everything from our capacity to obtain loans to our employment possibilities. In my role as a coach, I am committed to educating people about credit and advising them on how to raise their scores so they can live better. I've shared my story to encourage you to manage your credit and get assistance if necessary.

William Moore, COO of Generational Wealth Zone LLC, is a charismatic speaker and trainer with more than two decades' of experience as a certified credit counselor, strategist, and business credit coach helping clients address negative money behaviors and implement sound financial strategies.

www.coachwilliammoore.com

A PRESCRIPTION FOR A STRESS-FREE AND WORRY-FREE FINANCIAL LIFE

Dr. Lorie A. L. Nicholas

"I'm sorry, Ms. Nicholas, but we are unable to help you. Your credit scores are too low, and your debt-to-income ratio is too high. Since you do not have any money. you do not qualify for our loan modification program."

I must have heard this statement over a thousand times as I searched for help. I had been contacting banks and mortgage companies to get my mortgage loan locked into a fixed low-interest rate. I was one of millions of victims of the subprime mortgage economic downturn that occurred between 2007-2010. The crisis led to a severe economic recession, with banks closing down or being taken over by other banks and many businesses going bankrupt, while millions of people lost their job and homes. Mortgages had been extended to borrowers who would have had difficulty obtaining a mortgage otherwise, and many were now unable to pay the increased interest rates.

Back then, I never imagined that my life would be so upside down financially; I truly did not see this coming. I was living paycheck to paycheck, not realizing that I was heading for trouble. As long as the bills were paid, I thought everything was good and

I was handling my finances well. I didn't know it then, but I was about to find out that I had a lot to learn.

Everything hit the fan at once. I had experienced some personal setbacks that were beyond my control. Just when things could not get any worse, I received a letter from my mortgage company that my interest rate would increase next month. I had to read the letter twice to understand the technical language. My mortgage was going to increase by seven hundred dollars. Now, where was I going to get an extra seven hundred dollars by next month?

As I was dealing with my own dilemma, I began to hear of people whose payments increased by a thousand dollars. Families were losing their homes, and many were just walking away from them due to the jump in their interest rates and payments. It was painful to watch television and see people's belongings thrown out on the street as they were being evicted. I wondered if I would be next. I tried desperately to get help and refinance to a lower interest rate.

I may have had low self-esteem and a lack of confidence before, but with all that was happening to me, I began to fall into a deep depression. I felt as if everything was hopeless. All I kept hearing from the banks and mortgage companies was the same broken record: "We are not able to help you." One bank representative told me to stop paying my bills, and then "maybe" I might be able to get some assistance, but it was not a guarantee. Another mortgage program representative stated that with my debt to income ratio being at 95 percent, I needed to apply for food stamps so I could eat. She was even nice enough to locate some soup kitchens in my area.

As time went on, I struggled every month to make my payments. During the process, I encountered a problem with one of my mortgage payments. My delayed payment created a trickle effect on my credit card payments. This was around the time that the credit card companies had instituted new rules. Under these new guidelines, the credit card companies practiced the authority to double payments and increase interest rates for a person defaulting or missing a payment on another creditors account. With this new policy, my interest rates went from 12 percent and 15 percent to 25.99 percent and 39.99 percent. No matter how much I called the credit card companies requesting assistance from the representatives and their supervisors, no matter how long I had been a paying customer, I did not receive any help from the creditors. Eventually my persistence with one creditor led to the decision that they would close my account, stop additional interest from accumulating, and I would just need to pay off my balances. The other creditors remained inflexible.

Based on my observation of what was taking place in people's lives with their finances, I realized that debt is a heavy burden many people carry with them every day. The weight of these financial obligations can lead to anxiety, depression, and feelings of hopelessness. In some cases, there were news reports of people committing suicide. For me, being in debt was a constant source of stress and worry that affected every aspect of my life. I felt embarrassed and ashamed as a professional woman because I did not have it all together. I contemplated walking away from my apartment. I contemplated applying for bankruptcy. I had so many unanswered questions and no one to talk to.

After several more rejection phone calls with the banks, one day I was thinking about my situation. Although I had been praying for things to get better before, this time my prayers felt a bit stronger, with a purpose in mind. I also asked myself how I would help a friend in a similar situation. This helped me to reignite strength in my faith. I became determined that I was not going to let debt beat me—I was going to beat debt. I was also saddened by the stories of families who had physically lost their homes and wondered how we could all be of help to one another. I could understand and relate to their plight since I was on the building ledge as well, performing a balance act to avoid falling off the ledge into eviction or foreclosure. So many stories hit so close to home. I pondered the circumstances that led to all of us being in this mess. Although we could blame all this on various things, the bottom line was that we were in a financial crisis and needed to recover.

The steps I utilized to overcome my financial crisis were, believe it or not, the basic foundational components to money management that we all hear about but neglect to follow. If you are in debt and feeling overwhelmed, I want you to know that you are not alone. It Is possible to get out of debt and change your financial situation from a negative of living in debt to a positive of being able to save—but it takes time, effort, commitment, and dedication. Listed below are steps that everyone can follow. However, of more importance is your belief that things will work out. Continue to remain committed and determined to succeed. Don't give up on yourself, no matter what obstacles or roadblocks you encounter on your path. The following is my six-step approach of working toward a successful, stress-free, and worry-free financial life.

1. **Face your debt head-on.** People do not plan to fail; they fail to plan. In my twenty years of counseling clients, I have never met anyone who intentionally planned to fail at life. When it comes to financial matters, we must learn to plan and budget. The first phase is acknowledging that you have a problem and that you are ready to do something about it. You are no longer burying your head in the sand. As the first action step, face your debt head-on. Gather all your bills and write down all your current financial obligations. I made a list of every single expense. For credit card bills, I wrote down the total balance and minimum monthly payments due and the interest rates on each card. Given the current payments, I calculated how long it would take me to pay off all my expenses.

2. **Break through your barriers.** In order to overcome the obstacles in your path, you have to be determined and committed to

making a change in your life. You did not fall into debt overnight. It was a gradual process. Therefore, you need to realize that your debt will not go away overnight either, unless by some miracle you win the Mega Millions or Powerball. Write down all your incoming sources of funds each month. Be sure to include all paychecks you receive as well as alimony, child support, money received from retirement funds, investments, etc.

3. **Be conscious about where your money goes.** How many of you have ever left home with ten or twenty dollars and then, upon returning home, are unable to account for where the money went? It's very easy for money to slip away from us. It's important to be aware of how you are spending your money and what you are spending it on. With this in mind, calculate the differences between step 1 (your current monthly financial obligations) and step 2 (all incoming monthly funds). If your monthly income is equal to or more than your financial obligations, you should have enough money to cover your expenses. If your financial obligations are more than your current monthly income, there are some additional steps that need to be considered. Depending on the amount of the difference between the two monthly figures, determine whether there are resources that you can tap into make up for this difference (i.e., borrow money from family or friends, reduce interest rates on credit cards, work out payments of smaller amounts, obtain additional work to help increase incoming funds, etc.). Creating a budget is essential for getting out of debt and staying on track with your finances. You want to work toward developing a budget in which your income is able to equal and eventually surpass your expenditures. In order to do this, determine how to reduce your expenditures, which we will discuss in the next step.

4. **Reduce your expenditures.** This step involves stepping out of your comfort zone. At times we may find it hard to break away from our normal routines. We get comfortable keeping things

the way they are. This may not always be a healthy or adaptive way of coping with things. Depending on the situation, you might be required to step out of your comfort zone and get a little uncomfortable with the changes you need to make in your life. Make a log of your daily expenses for one or two months. Carefully review your expenditures and determine what types of things you can cut back on or eliminated. I reviewed all of my expenses to assess whether there were any expenses that could be reduced or eliminated. I reduced what I could, but for the most part, since there were no excess expenses like lattes or eating out, I did not have many daily expenses that could be reduced. But I could stop shopping for clothing. It's important to track your cash flow and know where your money goes.

5. **Transform negative thinking into positive energy.** It's not unusual to think negatively when faced with a crisis or unpleasant situation. I stated earlier how my situation left me feeling hopeless with low self-esteem and a lack of confidence. I tell my clients you have to get back up. It's when you do not get back up that you are throwing in the towel of defeat. I began transforming my negative thoughts into positive words and energy. I realized I was not alone in this situation; there were other resources I could utilize to help myself. I reviewed my resources of people I knew and companies I was connected to, and I ended up consulting with lawyers from a legal program I belonged to. As one of the services, the lawyers will write letters on your behalf. I had a lawyer write letters to the creditors that had still not responded to my requests for assistance. The results I received gratified me. My interest rates of 25.99 percent and 39.99 percent were dramatically reduced to 5.5 percent and 6 percent. With my new interest rates in effect, I recalculated how long it would take for me to pay off my revised current expenses. I began to feel more confident and a sense of hope. Throughout this process, I continued to review my income,

and I continued to monitor closely how I spent money and how I allocated my funds toward my bill payments. As I stayed on track with my plan, the balances reduced drastically. As I paid off each bill, I expressed gratitude and celebrated my blessings, not by spending money, but by being proud that I continued to stay the course and accomplished the improvement of my financial situation.

6. **Visualize oceans of prosperity—program your mind for success.** As I continued to successfully recover from debt, I decided it was time for me to start saving whatever money that I could. Although many financial advisors emphasize paying yourself first, at 10 percent of your monthly income, I had to start with what I could afford. Even as little as five dollars a week or a month is a start. Increase this amount as you are able. Whatever amount you decide, make sure you are able to be consistent on a regular basis. The money you set aside each month can then be utilized for emergencies, retirement, and other long term goals.

Squeezing the Lemonade Out of This Lemon

During this crisis, Habitat for Humanity found the families that were in their homes plagued with financial problems as a result of the economic downturn. As a volunteer for Habitat for Humanity, I was trained as a "Loan Ranger" to provide financial education so the families would not lose their homes. By this point, I had learned the steps I needed to apply to successfully navigate my way through my own dilemma. I was able to speak directly from personal experience, thereby helping other families to save their homes. From this experience, my passion for financial education was born.

I hope that by sharing my story and the six steps I utilized to turn my financial situation around, I have inspired you to realize that you too can triumphantly succeed in your financial recovery. Push beyond your limits and take immediate action. As you start this process, you will be able to reduce your financial stress and work toward creating a stress-free, worry-free financial life.

Dr. Lorie A. L. Nicholas has an extensive background in counseling, teaching, and research. She has presented at many conferences and has conducted a variety of workshops and trainings. Dr. Nicholas holds a doctorate in Clinical-Community Psychology and is a Certified Financial Education Instructor.

www.thefinancialrecoverydoctor.com

LIFE AFTER CORPORATE: MY JOURNEY TO COMMERCIAL MULTIFAMILY REAL ESTATE

Sonya Rocvil

This chapter is dedicated to my parents and my husband—my family, my tribe, my bedrock. I thank God for them.

My Fascination with Real Estate Investing

I was always fascinated by real estate. Maybe it's because I am from New York and have always been surrounded by buildings. In our annual trips over the holidays to our family in Brooklyn (when Brooklyn was not what it is today), I remember seeing so many abandoned buildings and people without homes. *How can this be?* I wondered. Housing is an essential need. Although there are many forms of real estate, I think residential real estate has always fascinated me the most. I feel very blessed to have grown up in a stable and safe home, and I think this is a foundation everyone should have.

As a Queens, New York, native, I am first generation. My parents are originally from Jamaica, West Indies. They came to this country, like many immigrant families, seeking a better life. As professionals in Jamaica and migrating to the United States, they instilled in me a sense of hard work and integrity.

My mother recognized quickly that raising a child here in the United States was going to be very different from raising one in Jamaica. I will never forget what she told me: "You have two things against you; you are Black, and you are a woman, and you must always do your best."

With that as my foundation, I did my best to do well in school. I got on the honor roll and earned a scholarship to undergrad school. I selected a career in accounting, through the guidance of one of my church mentors who told me that accounting was the language of business. I had an internship in undergrad in a financial services organization, and I decided to pursue a career in audit and get my CPA license. I then spent much of my career in financial services, going to school part-time to get an MBA while I worked full-time.

As I progressed through my career, I found that the skill set I developed in accounting, audit, and financial analysis aligned to the skill set needed to evaluate a deal, determine its value, and manage its ongoing success.

The Decision to Start My Own Company

I worked in financial services for over ten years. While I liked the people in my company and learned a tremendous amount, I had a hard time envisioning where I would go next in the company and what line of business I wanted to work in. While the company was excellent and there were many individuals supportive of me and my career, I was losing my passion for products and the business. Nevertheless, I stayed.

When I was in my thirteenth year at the company, I was told that my role was going away and I would be laid off, along with several members of my team. While this was hard news to take, I have to say it was a relief. I had to make a choice as to whether I would try to find another role in the company or go to another firm.

Then I realized I had another option. I could begin pursuing my passion and interest in real estate. I joined my local NYC REIA, as well as another New York-based real estate investing group. I got accepted into the Project REAP (Real Estate Associate Program), which focuses on diversity in commercial real estate. With all these pieces coming together, I decided to start my own company so I could invest in real estate. Starting the company wasn't hard, but I learned that functioning as a company is challenging. I always had one role in a particular job in the past. Suddenly I became the finance, marketing, CEO, human resources, and IT department all in one.

I had to figure out how to think about my business from many angles now, not just one. This took a long time for me to understand. Every time I thought I had it figured out, my business grew and changed, and I had to reshuffle and start again. I had to figure out which hat I needed to wear on a particular day and when I had to wear all the hats at the same time.

Working for Myself

I really like working for myself because I had more control of my time. However, you really have to be disciplined. I thought I was disciplined before I started working for myself, but I realized that I needed even more focus. When you have flexibility, you sometimes take on more than you should, especially if you are working from home.

For me, especially in the beginning when I had two very young children, I would tend to get sucked in to working around the house. When my children were infants, this was unavoidable. I received a lot of help from my family, especially my mother. I am not a neat freak at all, but I always wanted to put away the dishes and clean up. Thankfully, I have a great husband who does the laundry on the weekend! And while I must keep my workspace neat, I don't get obsessed with making sure everything is perfect around me. I've learned to focus on my business instead of cleaning the sink. I need to review deals, make decisions, and think about the next stages for my business instead of vacuuming. The flexibility of working from home allows me to choose my environment, and I realize that sometimes I have to get out of the house and work in another environment. Co-working spaces are great for this. I'm glad I have one nearby.

My motivation to succeed is rooted in being entrusted with other people's money; this really motivates me to do my best to make the best decisions to safeguard their money and make decisions that will optimize their investment dollars. It's so important to me that I help our investors achieve their goals and work to achieve the targets we've set.

One of the things that makes me unique is the way I approach investments. It really rests on three pillars: our investors, our customers (the residents that live in our properties), and the communities in which we invest. Taking a practical approach that focuses on of these pieces helps deliver the greatest impact for everyone. I typically invest in workforce housing communities. When we approach investing by looking at ways to improve the living environment and create value for our investors, customers, and our community, we get the best results.

I am frequently asked the following questions, and I'll share my answers and insights here:

When did you start investing in multifamily properties?

I started investing in multifamily properties by passively investing in other individual deals. I found people that I trusted and decided that I would invest in their deals. This gave me the opportunity to learn about different markets and build up my investment resume. I knew that when I was looking for multifamily deals,

I would have more credibility when I spoke to commercial real estate brokers if I had some investments properties, even if I was a partial owner.

As I started to build my portfolio of passive investments, I was able to leverage this in speaking with real estate investment brokers. It made me more credible and added to my resume as an investor. Several months after I started investing passively, a deal in my chosen market came across my desk. In modeling it out, the deal looked like a good opportunity. This very first deal has been the star of our portfolio. We raised the money with friends and family. It was challenging to get through this first raise, but it was a great deal for our investors, and we are proud of our performance and the impact we've had on the property and product we were able to deliver to our customers.

The term *asset management* comes up frequently in commercial real estate. What is this?

Asset management is often one of the most overlooked aspects of property ownership. This means that you take all the assumptions you've made about the property when you did your analysis and make them a reality. You may spend months negotiating and working on a deal to get it ready to close. Then, you will spend the next several years, or however long you hold the property, working with your property manager to make sure that your assumptions become reality. If you have investors, you must work the best that you can to deliver on your assumptions. This is the toughest part of the deal, because if you were too aggressive in your assumptions and did not raise enough money to cover your capital projects, or if you assumed that revenue was going to be higher or your costs were going to be lower, you are going to miss your number and be underfunded for your project.

In our company, asset management also includes investor relations. We have to determine how frequently we will make payouts to investors, as well as how often we will give them updates of the property's progress. We inform our investors of this up front to manage their expectations.

You have a family—how do you find the time to balance?

I have a full life. There are a lot of demands for the work I do. I have to travel to each property to make sure things are operating smoothly. However, there is some flexibility in my schedule that allows me to be there for my kids. There are many things I have been blessed with that help me get as much as I can done.

First of all, I have a very supportive husband. My husband was 1,000 percent behind me when I decided to make my career move. When I decided to leave corporate, we did not have children at the time. It was easier to manage our schedules. We took advantage of the time we had together to go on trips and visit friends abroad. I didn't realize it then, but the time we spent together before we had children really helped us to bond together after we had children. We had such great experiences, and the saying is really true: You don't really know someone until your travel with them. These experiences before becoming parents brought us closer together. We are fortunate that we share the same value system. Picking a life partner is just like picking a business partner in many ways. The values you share are what keep you grounded in the bigger picture and what you both want out of life.

My family—my mother especially—has been very supportive of us. When I travel, she comes over to help my husband and the children get ready in the morning. She helps with meals and packing bags and lunches. I am so grateful for her help. We live near our family, and this is super helpful.

Our community is a blessing, too. We met other families in our area at our children's school that we've really connected with. We work together with our neighbor to coordinate drop-offs, pickups, and play dates. We also have found some good babysitters in our area that we can rely on to help us out.

I also finally realized the areas in my business where I personally need help. There are some things I learned to outsource, and now I have a virtual team that I use for some aspects of my businesses, and this has really helped me. I plan to expand this outsourcing more to see what things I absolutely have to do versus what things can I systematize so I can delegate them to someone else.

I try to make time for things that help build regularity and rhythm in our lives. For example, I want to make sure I am reading to my daughter and my son every day, spending time with them during the week, and making time for them on the weekends. Also, I need to time with my husband and time for myself to think and recharge.

My husband introduced me to audiobooks. This has been life-changing.

When you own your own business, you have to build your tribe. You cannot do everything by yourself. Your tribe may be people you hire, but it has to be people you trust.

How can someone get started in real estate?

Real estate is a long-term play. I wish I could tell you that you could get started with no money down and no credit and become a millionaire in a month. That is not the case at all, however. The larger the deals, the more gain, but the more capital required to get the deal and the bigger the risk. You need to have a personal balance sheet that lenders will approve in order for you to secure a loan. You need to have relationships in the market you are working with so you have access to deals that you can analyze.

I've learned that you can do more with a very good partner than you can do by yourself. Don't be greedy. A percentage of something is better than 100 percent of nothing. You may take a little less money to close a deal, but you are building your resume and your credibility.

Real estate is a relationship business. Any relationship takes time to build. It may be years before you actually work with someone, but you should cultivate your relationships with brokers, lenders, property managers, local people in the market, and people in the network. If you are looking at a market other than the state where you live, you have to be there consistently enough to understand how the market works in that area.

I would start by really taking a hard look at your financial situation. Understand your credit and know what financial assets you bring to the table.

Find other people who share your common goals. Join real estate investment groups—probably more than one—to find other people with similar interests. Go to networking events and meet people. Your network is important. As one of my mentors says, your network is your net worth.

Know your value. You may not have a lot of money, but perhaps you are great at speaking with people and solving problems. Maybe you are great at gathering market information, synthesizing it, and coming up with recommendations and strategy. I learned to help busy professionals invest in multifamily apartments. I now also provide coaching services to assist individuals who want to purchase their own deals buy multifamily buildings.

Find people who are doing what you want to do. See how you can help them. Add value to other people.

Be patient. Building an empire takes time!

Sonya Rocvil is the principal and founder of Bedrock Real Estate Investors, which specializes in the acquisitions and asset management of multifamily apartments in the United States. She is a CPA and licensed real estate agent. A frequent guest on podcasts and webinars, Sonya lives with her husband and two children in Brooklyn, New York.

www.bedrockreinvestors.com

BREAKING BARRIERS: USING TECHNOLOGY FOR BUSINESS GROWTH

James Earl Thompson

"The first rule of any technology used in a business is that automation applied to an efficient operation will magnify the efficiency. The second is that automation applied to an inefficient operation will magnify the inefficiency."

—Bill Gates

It all began with a simple game of Tetris. You know, the one where you try to fit all the differently shaped blocks together to clear a line? As a child, I was obsessed with it. I spent hours playing it and trying to beat my high score on the Nintendo Game Boy my Auntie Pernaria and Cousin Gwen gave me.

Little did I know that game would become a metaphor for my journey from director in Corporate America to coach in private business. In the corporate world, there are countless pieces that must fit together perfectly to create a successful business. And just like in Tetris, it's all about strategy and systems.

I discovered my passion for electronics and futuristic technology during my undergraduate studies at North Carolina A&T, and this inspired me to go beyond my limits and take risks others wouldn't. I constantly challenged myself to expand my skill set. Despite trying to remain unnoticed in my manufacturing management class, my professor saw potential in me and pushed me to be the director of operations for our class project. This experience propelled me into entrepreneurship, leading me to successfully complete my bachelor's in Electronics Computer Technology and then pursue a master's in Networking & Telecommunications at Purdue University.

I started my corporate career as a field supervisor in wireless communication before finding my passion in programming during the rise of the internet and automation use. As a field supervisor in the pre-Y2K era, I used manual processes to manage multiple job sites and technicians. Post-Y2K, I jumped on the wave and entered the programming industry as automation became increasingly necessary for tasks such as scheduling and emails. During that time, I worked on high-profile projects that led to the development of VOIP and witnessed the rise of bots taking over repetitive tasks. This allowed larger corporations to downsize while still experiencing profit growth. Smaller companies, however, saw little-to-no growth due to their fear of technology and a lack of resources.

Moving from supervisor to manager to director, I continued to see the way processes and automation positively impacted profits as well as how outsourcing made managing projects resources easier. I began exploring ways to make corporate-level processes, automation, and technology affordable for solopreneurs, enabling them to generate similar profits with fewer resources. This inspired me to offer coaching services and strategies for business processes and automation at a more accessible level, empowering small business owners who lacked education on cutting-edge technology to experience growth comparable to that of larger corporations or the " big dogs."

Being a product of STEM (Science, Technology, Engineering, and Mathematics), my vision has always been education and implementation of technology to improve our way of life.

My success in the IT and security industries stemmed from hands-on experience with systems and processes, and this led to coaching large companies to near perfection using processes and systems. I began coaching solopreneurs, and quickly learned that balancing private coaching while working a corporate job was challenging. I persisted, however, and used automating and outsourcing to free up my time because I still required my corporate salary to fund my coaching business. Automating and outsourcing was crucial because being both a director and solopreneur demands time efficiency. Automation and outsourcing ultimately allowed me to transition from a director to a full-time strategist and coach, changing my life for the better.

All businesses need processes to function, but automation is what improves the efficiency of these processes. Just like that Tetris game, all the pieces need to fit together perfectly in order for the business to grow.

As a solopreneur, it's easy to get bogged down in day-to-day tasks and overlook profitable opportunities. After months of searching, I came up with the solution: Automation can improve processes and save valuable time. And now, using the powerful automated systems and processes I've developed over twenty years for larger companies, I create affordable solutions for small businesses and solopreneurs.

It has been a long journey from director in corporate America to coach, but I wouldn't trade it for the world. My passion for technology and processes has enabled me to bridge the gap between corporate strategy and automation while teaching business owners how they can leverage them to their advantage. So, whether you're just starting out or are looking to capitalize on automation's benefits, I'm here to provide guidance and help you take your business to the next level.

Are you ready to accelerate your business with automation? Let's see how automation can improve your specific business.

Automation Is the Key

For solopreneurs, time is a precious commodity, as they often do the majority of work themselves. Automation is the key to efficiency and success, saving time and energy. With automation, solopreneurs can focus on important business aspects such as planning, problem-solving, and building relationships with clients. In fact, according to Accenture, innovations such as AI chatbots can increase productivity by 40 percent.[1] This is because automation eliminates repetitive tasks, reducing the workload on employees and allowing them to focus on more critical tasks that require human creativity and problem-solving skills.

Furthermore, automation improves accuracy, reduces errors, and increases overall efficiency. It also ensures consistency and standardization across all business processes. Therefore, it is essential for businesses, regardless of their size, to embrace automation as a key driver of success. With the right automation tools and strategies in place, businesses can increase profits, win back valuable time, and improve their overall operations. As Bill Gates said, "Automation is not a choice anymore; it is a necessity."[2]

We live in an age when computers can do virtually anything for us. But you probably do not know just how much help automated programs can be. Marketing automation uses software and web-based services to execute and manage marketing tasks, whereas email marketing requires automating subscriptions, list organization, and message broadcasts. With automated programs, business owners can streamline operations and achieve success.

---

[1] "Boost Your Business's Productivity by 40% with Artificial Intelligence," *Business Focus Magazine*, March 3, 2023, https://www.businessfocusmag-azine.com/2023/03/03/boost-your-businesss-productivity-by-40-with-artifi-cial-intelligence/.
[2] Bill Gates quoted in "32 of the Best AI and Automation Quotes," *AKASA*, October 18, 2022, https://akasa.com/blog/automation-quotes/.

21 Ways to Automate Marketing

1. **Schedule Posts and Tweets**—To achieve successful social media marketing, consistency in posting is key. Automating your schedule can save time and ensure regular posting. However, it's also important to manually post time-sensitive content, such as commenting on breaking news, and respond to comments personally. Set up notifications or delegate someone on your team to manage social media activity.

2. **Visitor Tracking**—Visitor tracking is crucial to determine the effectiveness of your online marketing efforts. With automated programs, you can analyze visitor behavior, identifying who visits your site and which pages and content they engage with. This data can help you create a better user experience on your website and help you to improve pages that are viewed briefly and then abandoned.

3. **Upsell Opportunities**—Automating upsell opportunities can save time and offer personalized deals to customers based on their behavior. Email marketing is a great way to accomplish this. Build an email list and ask customers to opt-in to receive offers at the point of sale. Autoresponder email programs allow you to preload messages and send them at intervals of time chosen by you. Use this service to send relevant and enticing offers with links to the exact product a particular customer may be interested in.

4. **Offer Educational Tools**—Automated email software can be used to offer educational opportunities to subscribers. Create an email course with lessons that are sent automatically on a set schedule, such as one lesson per week. The lessons should build on one another and teach subscribers how to do something, such as setting up an ecommerce business or building a website. You can offer the course for free to

customers as a thank-you gift or as a lead magnet to add potential customers in exchange for their contact details. Providing valuable educational content builds relationships that can lead to future sales.

5. **Searching for Content**—To keep an audience engaged in online marketing, a consistent flow of content is necessary. While you may create some content, sharing others' content such as news articles, infographics, and blog posts can also be beneficial. Notification programs can provide relevant content for you to sift through and share. This saves time that would be spent manually searching for content to share.

6. **Checking Your Work**—You can automate the crucial process of editing, checking grammar, and spelling. Spelling and grammar mistakes decrease trust and make you look unprofessional, damaging your reputation. With automated editing programs, you can identify lengthy sentences, simplify text, and use dictionaries, thesauruses, and other helpful tools to improve your writing.

7. **Customer Loyalty Programs**—Customer loyalty programs are post-sale programs that incentivize customers with bonuses and deals for regular purchases. One common example is a points card, where customers accumulate points that can be redeemed for goods or discounts. Automating customer loyalty programs with online systems simplifies tracking customer purchases and rewards. You can choose from a variety of loyalty programs such as raffles, exclusive offers, and partnership promotions.

8. **Website Testing**—Streamlining and perfecting your website is achievable through split-testing and multivariate testing. By running two or more versions of the same website with slight changes made to elements, you can track which elements

drive sales and engagement. Automating website testing is recommended, as it can test more variables, and deliver a wider range of data. Automated programs can even provide suggestions on how to improve your site.

9. **Renewal Reminders**—Automated renewal reminders are an efficient way to remind customers of expiring memberships, contracts, or subscriptions. Not only do reminders help build relationships with customers, but they also offer valuable marketing opportunities by providing a touchpoint to remind customers of the unique value you offer or to mention new deals and offers.

10. **Post Once Everywhere**—Social media dashboards and other automation programs simplify multi-platform posting by allowing you to post once across all your platforms. Dashboard programs can automate additional aspects of social media marketing such as analytics and follower engagement.

11. **Thank-You Messages**—Sending thank-you messages to customers after sign-ups, social media likes, and purchases can go a long way in building customer relationships. Automating these is simple, and you can use email marketing for new sign-ups or an automated confirmation message after purchases.

12. **Manage Your Content**—Using a content management system (CMS) is essential for automating content creation, management, and publishing. These systems offer numerous automation options, such as scheduling regular content publishing without manual work. Additionally, CMSs help organize and manage teams in one central location.

13. **Automate Your Outsourcing**—Hiring a team of freelancers can be tedious and time-consuming, but using freelancer websites can automate the process. Sites manage hiring

paperwork, payment guarantees, and escrow for payments, making it easier to hire virtual workers.

14. **Lead Scoring**—Lead scoring programs use automation to qualify leads more accurately than humans can. These programs analyze demographic information as well as customer actions such as pages viewed, content consumed, or content downloaded to determine which leads are worth nurturing. Automation software goes beyond evaluating basic demographic information alone.

15. **Spy on the Competitors**—Automated monitoring programs can help you stay up-to-date on competitors, and automatic alerts help track the competitions' social media mentions and website changes. You can also subscribe to RSS feeds and email lists to keep tabs on competitor emails and blog content.

16. **Give Webinars**—Webinars are a great way to reach people globally, and many aspects can be automated, such as registering attendees, sending invitation reminders, special features for the event, and more. Automation makes it easy to hold a successful online seminar with attendees from all over the world.

17. **Automated Payments**—Automated payments provide a secure way to transfer money online with ease. Shopping carts on ecommerce websites make it easy for customers to purchase items, while automated payment solutions such as scanning a QR code or logging in are even quicker.

18. **Landing Pages**—Landing pages are designed to run on autopilot and can generate leads without any effort from you. They come with a sign-up form for visitors to enter their contact details, usually accompanied by an incentive such as a free gift. Once created, the page simply requires traffic for it to be effective.

19. **SEO Automation**—SEO automation is a great way to optimize your content. Automated programs can help you find, test, and analyze keywords so you can choose the most effective ones for your marketing strategy. You can use these programs to get real-time statistics on search volume, and the data from these programs can offer insights into a competitor's SEO strategy.

20. **Talk, Don't Type**—Voice recognition is a great way to speed up the process of writing content. Programs like this take some training and require some editing, but they can be helpful if typing isn't your strength or you are pressed for time. To get started, you can create an outline of what you want to cover in the article and then fill in the details as you talk. Editing parts of it later ensures accuracy and clarity.

21. **Coming Up with Ideas**—When you're stuck for ideas, automated programs can help you brainstorm and generate content topics and titles. They can also help you organize your ideas through mind mapping or store them for future reference.

To conclude, the world of automation has changed dramatically in recent times. It's now very economical (sometimes even free) and incredibly simple to implement. Anyone in the business world can benefit from the different automation technologies and tools available, which can save an enormous amount of time. As a solopreneur, explore the different automation programs and processes to identify the ones that can help you streamline processes and duplicate tasks to increase your profits. Automation technologies and tools make it easy to quickly carry out routine tasks in an efficient way, thus freeing you up for more important responsibilities.

If you're a bit intimidated by technology, don't worry—it's easy to get started. Start by automating one task at a time, and once you're comfortable and are seeing results, scale up to the next one. Soon you'll realize how automation saves you time and helps impact your business growth positively.

With a strategic plan in place and the right documentation to back it up, you'll have the knowledge to create a solid foundation on which your business can grow. I can help you identify what automation works best for your specific needs, allowing you to delegate tasks so you benefit from increased profits, reduced stress, and improved freedom as you drive your business forward.

James Earl Thompson is an entrepreneur and marketing and business systems strategist. His passion is coaching busy small business owners and entrepreneurs to maximize their resources, increase their profits, and grow their business using technology. He is a recognized leader in the education and implementation of IT solutions, business processes, marketing automation, and effective marketing campaign development.

www.coachjamesearlthompson.com

JOURNEY TO BECOMING DEBT-FREE

Shanita P. Williamson

My journey to becoming debt-free began with my decision to change my relationship with money. It was a necessary change because having a low credit score affects everything—interest rates, employment options, and even where you live. This was the case for me in the summer of 1999. I look back now and realize that my finances directly reflected what was happening in my personal life, and this dragged on for years.

I regret not taking the sound advice of an upperclassman when I applied for my first credit card in 1994. I remember her warning me to leave those credit cards alone or I would regret it. However, low self-esteem and trying to please people were just the beginning of my demise. A year later, I used my credit card to purchase two additional Bad Boy Entertainment tickets for a concert in Upstate New York and never got reimbursed from two of my former classmates.

The biggest financial hit during my third year of college was using credit cards and cash to travel to the UK in May 1997 to meet someone I met just months earlier. This man was almost ten years older than me and became abusive toward me during my visit. I unwisely converted my American currency to British pounds, giving him a small lottery win of eighty pounds for numbers that I picked at a local off-license (the US equivalent of a convenience or liquor store), where I purchased alcoholic drinks and cigarettes for him. I'll never forget that off-license because that's where the last of my hard-earned money was spent during my twelve days in Southeast London.

My father never told me that a man is supposed to pay for a date. Instead I was told that "It's not what they want, but what they can get." Well, that was certainly the case in my unstable relationship at the time; the cost of a plane ticket, going out to eat, and partying at a rave in London were all funded by me. My trip overseas was followed by a heated exchange of words and a family fallout that ended with me being broke, in debt, and homeless.

This experience in the fall of 1997 changed the way I viewed the world, and whatever naivety and idealism side of me died that year. Years later when I looked at photos before, during, and after my trip, I looked like a different person. It took decades before I recovered emotionally, mentally, and financially. I went through shock and was so devastated that I could barely focus on my studies. I had to seek help by attending therapy because I was having a difficult time.

By winter break, I was staying at a friend's house. I started opening more lines of credit and started to shop as part of my retail therapy just to look the part and mask the depression. During my last spring break, two months before graduation, I was sitting on a pressure cooker because of the ongoing stress of finding employment outside of Boston. I crashed at a friend's apartment in Harlem and attended a local college job fair. We had plans to live together, but I called it off after canceling a second interview with Met Life at the World Trade Center. When I graduated from college in June 1999 and wanted to relocate, my other employment options in New York City were limited due to credit issues, and I had to move back to Boston.

I went through one of the worst transitions from being a college student to trying to keep a job due to personal issues at home. The lack of emotional and financial support was real. I was on my own and trying to figure out life in my early twenties when I needed guidance. I lost a few jobs before I landed full-time employment three years after graduation, but not before cleaning up charge-offs, bank overdrafts, and debts to the state and the IRS for late tax filing.

Years later, I could hold a steady job, but I was depressed, frustrated, angry, and had a lot of emotional baggage. A colleague from the Tri-State area who visited me in Boston on a business trip sensed that I had a lot going on and recommended that I watch *The Secret* DVD. I took her advice and started focusing on what I wanted. I thought about a time in my life when I was in a happy place and remembered spending time with my grandfather, an entrepreneur in Queens. Within six years, although I still lived in Boston, I got to experience a piece of New York.

In July 2016, I attended a three-day seminar in East Elmhurst Queens with a team of entrepreneurs. I was determined to be where the people were running business in the mecca of all places. Because of my focus and my ability to network and connect with others, I was surrounded by entrepreneurs, celebrity attorneys, and public figures in New York City. At that event, I even met one of the co-authors of *The Secret*, Loral Langemeier.

My journey to becoming debt-free began when a colleague from Brooklyn introduced me to Attorney Teresa Martin, Esq. Around that time, I had a friend from Boston who was working in the music industry and living in the Bronx, so I started coming to New York City more often, hoping to eventually relocate. I enjoyed networking with new faces and attending events in Manhattan and Brooklyn. At one after-work mixer I attended in Manhattan, a woman shared her crab cakes with me. I wondered why, but I love food, so I gladly accepted. My colleague from Brooklyn gave me this woman's contact information a few months later, and it was attorney Teresa R. Martin. I went to her law office before attending another event in Manhattan, and we ended up hanging out for over two hours.

Teresa just happened to be a foreclosure defense attorney. She taught me about debt management and credit restoration and referred me to a colleague from New Jersey, who helped me to settle some of my debts going as far back as college. I eventually traveled with Teresa's Las Vegas, Nevada, team in 2009.

By 2016 I was working two jobs and traveling to New York City every two or three months. Privately I had a lot of things going on, but a part of me knew I was destined to have a better life, and I was motivated to get myself in a better space. In the Tri-State area, I was introduced to well-established colleagues, which was a little intimidating. I would think, *Everyone else has their life in order, and I'm still trying to get it together financially.*

During this time, I still was broke, depressed, and had bad credit. At events, when the topic of finances and investments came up, I was too embarrassed to speak because that was not an option for me based on my credit score. At one point, I was in a panic because a creditor filed for collection, and I had to appear in court. I remember looking around and thinking, *This is no longer the kind of life for me.*

My mentor Teresa and I had a few heart-to-heart conversations over the years. One of the most important ones that was a pivotal financial moment in my life was when she recommended that I downsize my one-bedroom apartment and build an emergency fund. She said, "Shanita, you are on your own, and if something happens, you need to prepare. The money you spend on Whole Foods on your lunch break should be put into a do-not-touch fund. What will happen to you if you end up out of work?"

I ran to the bank the next day just before it closed. I put aside five hundred dollars a month while renting a room in an apartment for two years, and when the owner sold the property, I had twenty thousand dollars in cash, and my credit score was 750. My mentor helped me find hidden money in my bank account, as she would say. I am forever grateful for someone looking in from the outside to show me this was a serious matter because my circumstances and family dynamics were dire.

A different circle of people finally surrounded me, and the motivation to get it together became a reality through perseverance and hard work. Much of my time was spent in the Tri-State area, and I could travel there regularly and still save money because of Teresa's advice. Last year I went to Lower Manhattan and passed the New York State real estate salesperson exam.

Today, my money, credit, and spending habits have changed. I have a network and a support system. I have learned to live below my means and have built an emergency fund. The conference calls with my team are motivational. I am proud of my progress and am ready to build on it. Challenges in life happen, but I've learned that the extracurricular activity known to folks going through depression as "retail therapy" is not recommended and can land you in hot water. It would be more beneficial to talk to an actual therapist instead of your local retailer while spending money.

I'm now in a good place where I know my credit utilization and debt-to-income ratio. I want to increase my net worth before entering into any investment opportunities in the near future, and I plan to do so with the help of my team. I occasionally have had to say no to major purchases as well as no to a few people, which only means not now—and that's okay because I know by saying no I'm better off financially.

I definitely look forward to being a consultant to others who are in the same place financially where I once was. I still love watching Teresa's *Enjoy Your Legacy Promo* in order to stay focused and not get cooked in the microwaved society where you must have everything now, as mentioned in that video footage. You don't need to make a depreciating purchase such as a car or expensive pair of shoes. Unlike real estate, there is no return on your unnecessary investment.

I must reiterate that this journey has not been easy. It takes courage to pull yourself away from your old crowd and find a new squad who can help you break unhealthy habits so you can change your life. My advice is to seek people who are doing well financially and ask them how they got there. Most likely, they were in the same place as you at some point and took steps to make improvements. Consider downsizing your home and get a second job while trying to rebuild your credit and build a cash reserve for your business. Cut down on takeout orders and restaurants and prepare home-cooked meals. There is no sense in trying to keep up with everyone else with no savings in your bank account; this advice can save you hundreds and even thousands of dollars.

If you've had a few setbacks, made some financial mistakes, and have some personal issues, it's all about forgiving yourself and celebrating the small successes while working toward your financial goal. Get a journal, write, and take notes over time to reflect on how far you have come. And be proud of your progress!

I encourage you to set an example because it all starts with you. If you have children, do not withdraw your retirement funds for their education. Start teaching them financial literacy at a young age so they can be set for life. Set up a trust fund for your children if you have the financial means. If your children are of college age, encourage them to budget and not spend their money on people who eventually will be nothing more than former classmates and associates. Talk to your daughters about not financially funding a partner, especially while working and going to school. Teach her to protect her ass and her assets because she will have depleted funds when he is off with the next girl.

Stress the importance of maintaining a good credit score because job recruiters look at entry-level employees' scores. You want to be on the top of their list, not the bottom. As Loral Langemeier stated on the Dr. Phil show, "You can run from creditors, but you can't run from a credit score."

I look forward to assisting others with becoming financially fit and debt-free by becoming a financial consultant and incorporating that into my real estate business in New York, Massachusetts, and Rhode Island. In addition, I would like to assist people in debt management, helping them to decide when to buy a home and how to be financially prepared to do so. People need to know about not making major purchases like financing a vehicle or applying for additional lines of credit that can negatively affect a mortgage loan application so they are not blindsided when a loan officer issues an embarrassing rejection letter.

I would like to collaborate with other partners to teach financial literacy. Those partnerships might include local banks. I am focused on education, which is more effective as a group effort and executed by a team dedicated to a holistic approach to helping individuals. It's very important to get to the cause of a person's financial problems and develop a plan that suits their individual needs. As part of a team, I would like to help individuals build their credit and improve their finances so they are set for life.

My story is a lesson on how not to spend and instead how to make necessary adjustments regarding one's lifestyle and relationship with money. I am thankful for the opportunity to spend time in the Tri-State area with a mentor such as Teresa R. Martin Esq. It took me a lot of time and effort to pull myself out of a dark space and make some changes, and now I would like to team up with our many colleagues in the mission of prioritizing financial literacy.

Shanita P. Williamson lives in Boston and is a member of REIA NYC. She is in the process of obtaining her license to sell real estate in Massachusetts, New York, and Rhode Island. She is working on her autobiography and is part of the Massachusetts College of Liberal Arts Oral History Project.

www.shanitawilliamson.com

Printed in the USA
CPSIA information can be obtained
at www.ICGtesting.com
CBHW030346171023
1333CB00001BC/4